Misconception

OTHER BOOKS BY ANGELA HUNT

Collaborative Titles

Why I Stayed (with Gayle Haggard)

Don't Bet Against Me! (with Deanna Favre)

Idoleyes: My New Perspective on Faith, Fat & Fame
(with Mandisa)

Heavenly Crowns
(with Heather Whitestone McCallum)

Listening with My Heart
(with Heather Whitestone McCallum)

Let God Surprise You
(with Heather Whitestone McCallum)

Novels:

Let Darkness Come

The Face

The Elevator

Doesn't She Look Natural?

She Always Wore Red

She's in a Better Place

Uncharted

A Time to Mend

The Novelist

The Truth Teller

Unspoken

The Awakening

The Debt

The Canopy

The Pearl

The Note

The Justice

The Immortal

The Proposal

For more information about Angela Hunt,
please visit www.angelahuntbooks.com.

Misconception

*One Couple's Journey
from Embryo Mix-Up
to Miracle Baby*

Paul and Shannon Morell
with Angela Hunt

HOWARD BOOKS
A DIVISION OF SIMON & SCHUSTER, INC.

New York · Nashville · London · Toronto · Sydney

Published by Howard Books, a division of Simon & Schuster, Inc.
1230 Avenue of the Americas, New York, NY 10020

Misconception © 2010 Paul and Shannon Morell

Library of Congress Control Number: 2010008457

ISBN 978-1-4391-9361-7
ISBN 978-1-4391-9754-7 (ebook)

10 9 8 7 6 5 4 3 2 1

HOWARD colophon is a registered trademark of Simon & Schuster, Inc.

Manufactured in the United States of America

For information regarding special discounts for bulk purchases, please contact:
Simon & Schuster Special Sales at 1-866-506-1949 or business@simonandschuster.com.

The Simon & Schuster Speakers Bureau can bring authors to your live event.
For more information or to book an event, contact the Simon & Schuster Speakers Bureau at 1-866-248-3049 or visit our website at www.simonspeakers.com.

Edited by Cindy Lambert

Scripture quotations are taken from the Holy Bible, New Living Translation, copyright © 1996. Used by permission of Tyndale House Publishers, Inc., Wheaton, Illinois 60189. All rights reserved.

This work reflects the authors' present recollections of their experiences over a period of months. Certain names and identifying characteristics have been changed and/or omitted. Though every attempt has been made to depict conversations as accurately as possible, others may recall events differently.

For our children, Ellie, Megan, and Logan,
and to the unborn babies
we were not able to hold in this life;
and to Sean and Carolyn Savage,
for delivering to us the precious gift of our son.

Contents

Misconception

Introduction

There is probably nothing more private for a couple, more personal, than making decisions about reproduction. At least that is how Paul and I always felt. We have always been intensely private about such matters. Even close family and dear friends were not privy to our struggles with infertility or our decision about turning to in vitro fertilization, using our own eggs and sperm, to build our family.

Before September 2009, if you'd told us that we would reluctantly be featured on national television and plastered across headlines as the victims of a rare in vitro fertilization mistake, we would have been horrified at the thought. Quite frankly, as our very personal nightmare unfolded in the public eye, we were more than horrified. We were shell-shocked, embarrassed, confused, and overwhelmed.

So why would two very private people expose their personal health information to the public and write a book about how their baby ended up inside another woman's womb?

Because through our ordeal we have discovered so many misconceptions.

We have had to face misconceptions of our own about in vitro. Though we believed we were well-informed before we proceeded, we have learned much more about the ins and outs, processes and complexities of in vitro than we ever imagined.

We've become aware of misconceptions of other couples who, in considering in vitro for themselves, are turning to our story with questions and fears.

We have encountered misconceptions on the part of family and friends—our own and those of other infertile couples—who care and want to offer support and empathy, but find themselves confused and reluctant to pry.

And finally, we find ourselves face-to-face with misconceptions of the public, wanting to understand what happened—how and why—and, maybe most important, how such errors can be avoided in the future. The scrutiny of the public is also driven by the highly controversial questions of when life begins, when infertility treatments and procedures cross the line of moral ethics, and when assisting in conception becomes tampering with God's divine will. We are not theologians or medical ethicists. We are not setting ourselves up as authorities on these issues. We are simply one couple who wanted to build a family of their own, and whose story has become a touchstone for all who are debating such topics. Our hope is that in exposing our misconceptions, our questions, our discoveries, and our experiences, our story will shed light on these critically important issues.

We have witnessed how a single careless error can have life-changing consequences. We have learned some important lessons and gained valuable insights. And perhaps the most life-changing benefit of all, we have realized that God was working behind the scenes and continues to do so, bringing his plans to pass and answering our prayers—even when we find it hard to accept what is happening.

So though we are not at all comfortable in the spotlight, since we find ourselves here, we do not want our pain or experience to be wasted or our joys and gratitude to go uncelebrated. It is our hope and prayer that in telling our story many misconceptions can be cleared away, leaving nothing but the truth.

Chapter One

Like Any Other Day

The seventeenth of February 2009 began like any other day. The alarm went off at the usual hour, but I hit the snooze button three times, delaying wakefulness for as long as possible. I opened my eyes to see Paul still sleeping soundly and tiptoed out of the room. I'd been up with our daughter Megan during the night, and sunrise had come much too soon.

I had condensed my morning regimen to a bare-bones routine, but no matter how I planned ahead, nothing ever went smoothly. When I caught a few extra minutes of sleep, I could jump out of bed, slide into the shower, and dress—tossing my makeup bag into my purse, kissing the girls, and grabbing a cup of coffee as I went out the door.

That morning I took the same route I always drove to work, but traffic seemed more sluggish than usual. As always, I found myself frustrated with slower drivers who dawdled and stoplights that turned red when I approached. After turning on my favorite local talk radio, I put on my lipstick and sipped coffee as I sat at red lights, glancing around to see several other drivers wrapping their hands around their coffee cups. We were all trying to stay warm and awake.

Once I got to the middle school where I taught eighth grade, I went to my room and dropped my bulging purse on my desk. Almost immediately, I noticed that the message light on my classroom telephone was blinking. Who might be calling so early? Usually people only call the teacher when there's a problem, so I assumed it was one of my students' parents calling with a concern.

Postponing the inevitable, I walked around my L-shaped desk and hung up my coat. I pulled out my chair and slid into it, then sighed and picked up the phone. The automated voice told me I had two messages, so I pressed the button to play the first.

My heart skipped a beat when I heard the voice of a nurse from my fertility clinic. The doctor would like to talk to me, she said, so could I please call the office as soon as possible?

I rested the phone against my shoulder, thinking. I hadn't been to the fertility clinic in years, though I had an appointment scheduled for the next week. But why would the doctor want to speak to me now?

But there was another message. I pressed the button, expecting to hear from a parent, but I heard the nurse yet again, repeating the same message.

So . . . the doctor *really* wanted to talk to me. The nurse spoke in a calm voice, yet a note of urgency underlined her words. I didn't have much time to ponder the reason for the call because just then the morning bell sounded. I stepped into the hallway to supervise the oncoming rush of kids, but I couldn't get the odd message out of my mind. Maybe the doctor wanted to ask a few questions in light of my upcoming appointment. Maybe he wanted to tell me about a new development in procedure. This had to be good news . . . didn't it?

Fortunately, first period was my planning hour. After the tardy bell rang, I dialed the clinic. The nurse thanked me for calling and said my doctor would really like to speak to me, but he would be in surgery all day. Could he call me later in the afternoon, around four?

"Absolutely," I told her. "He can reach me during my lunch hour or after three thirty p.m."

She said she'd relay the information. Overcome with curiosity, I asked, "Do you know why he wants to speak with me?"

"No," she answered, and at that point a nagging doubt entered my mind. During my first in vitro process, which resulted in the birth of healthy twin girls, I had never spoken with the doctor over the phone. He always relayed instructions through his nurses, and they called me. The fact that he wanted to speak to me directly was . . . odd.

When second period began, I tried to keep my mind on my lessons as I taught American history to my energetic eighth graders. During my lunch hour I received another message from the clinic nurse—the doctor's surgeries were running late, and, by the way, he would like to speak with me in person, not over the phone. Could I come to his office later in the evening?

More curious than ever, I called the nurse again. "I'd be happy to come to the office. What time?" I asked, thinking that the arrangement would work out well. I'd been planning to take my girls with me next week so they could meet the doctor, but if we saw him tonight, I wouldn't have to take the girls next week. Before hanging up, I blurted out a question: "Should I bring my husband with me?"

"That would be a good idea."

I hung up the phone and wondered why the doctor was in such a hurry to speak with us.

After school, I called Paul to tell him about our appointment. As usual, he remained unflappable, not at all alarmed. We discussed what we could have for dinner that would be quick and easy, and decided on spaghetti.

Once I arrived at home, we received another phone call from the fertility clinic—the doctor was stuck in traffic and running late. Could we postpone the meeting by about thirty minutes?

"Sure, no problem," I told the nurse, relieved that I'd have an extra half hour to feed the girls. "We'll be there."

I was actually looking forward to bundling up the girls and taking them to the doctor's office—he had been my physician during our first in vitro cycle. This proud mama wanted him to see Megan and Ellie and know how happy he'd made us nearly three years before.

We ate quickly, though I didn't have much of an appetite. Then, because the girls' clothes were covered in spaghetti, I changed their outfits and we loaded them into the car.

Megan wanted to know where we were going.

"We're going to see my doctor."

"Your doctor? Don't you feel good?"

"I'm fine. It's just for a brief appointment."

On the way, the girls chattered away with Paul, leaving me with plenty of time to think. My thoughts kept drifting toward the clinic. I was dying to know what the doctor wanted to discuss, but I told myself to be patient—we'd be there soon enough, and then we'd hear whatever he had to say. In only a matter of minutes, the big mystery would be solved.

The sun had already set, and the facility's parking lot was nearly empty when we pulled in. Only a few lights burned inside the windows.

Mixed feelings surged within me as I studied the clinic building. I hadn't visited the practice since my last appointment when I was eight weeks pregnant with the girls.

Paul and I each unbuckled one of the girls from their car seats and hoisted them onto our hips. We walked forward and found the front door ajar, undoubtedly propped open for us. The waiting room stood empty, the magazines neatly stacked on the end tables. A single lamp burned at the check-in window, but no one emerged to greet us. I walked up to the counter and waited a minute or two, then decided to sit down. After five phone calls, someone had to be expecting us.

How nice, I thought, *for the doctor to meet with us at night.* We sat for about ten minutes, spending most of that time trying to get the girls to sit down and stop climbing on the furniture and shuffling the magazines.

Finally the nurse came out to talk to us. We chatted about the girls for a minute or two, then she motioned us forward, ready to lead us to the doctor's private office. Though she smiled the entire time, faint lines of strain puckered the skin of her forehead. Those faint lines sent a shiver of unease through me—why, exactly, had we been invited to this unconventional meeting?

Paul and I greeted my doctor from his office doorway, introducing him to our toddlers. He stood up and shook our hands, then greeted the girls. "These are the twins," he said. "Oh, they are beautiful."

I smiled. "That's right. You've never seen them before."

"No, we usually only see photos, so this is nice. Now, if you'll please step into my office so we can talk . . ."

The doctor was gracious and kind, but I couldn't help thinking that he looked exhausted.

"I've had a long day and I've just finished a complicated surgery." He gestured to a pair of chairs. "Why don't you have a seat?"

Still wearing my coat, I dropped into the nearer chair. Paul sat on the other, gathering the girls around him. The doctor moved behind his desk. "Thank you for coming in," he said, sinking into his seat. He paused, shuffled a few papers, then looked directly at the two of us. "I thought it would be best to speak to you in person rather than over the phone."

Alarm bells began to clang in my brain, nearly blocking out my awareness of the girls clambering behind me. What was this about? I didn't have to wait long for the answer.

He hesitated for a moment and dropped his head, then took a deep breath and looked me in the eye. "I'm so sorry, Shannon, but there's been a terrible incident in our lab." The doctor's voice became darker and grimmer. He took a deep breath. "Your embryos have been thawed."

I blinked as I absorbed the news. I could see stress on the doctor's face, so I knew this matter was serious. Thawed embryos . . . meant our babies were dead. All six of the tiny embryos that had been stored so we could soon expand our family. Some kind of massive power outage must have struck the storage lab, and probably thousands of frozen embryos had died. . . . All those poor families!

I gasped. No wonder the doctor looked worried.

Little did I know that within the space of a few moments, I would wear that same expression myself . . . and I would continue to wear it for months. For reasons I could not understand, God took responsibility for our embryos out of our hands and placed it instead into the hands of strangers.

Sitting in that office, I looked at my trembling hands pressed against my knees, then looked up at Paul. In that moment we both realized that our lives were about to spiral out of our control.

Chapter Two

Love, Marriage, and . . .

Love, marriage, and motherhood had never been my ultimate goal. I wasn't one of those girls who falls in love during high school and marries right after graduation. I met Paul when I was twenty-three and assumed I'd eventually marry, but I was in no rush. I had high expectations, and good men were hard to find.

In July 2002, Paul and I married in Croswell, Michigan. We had known each other nine years, and we were older than the average first-time bride and groom: I was thirty-two and Paul was thirty-one. But we would have the rest of our lives to be together and create a family.

Since we were in our early thirties at the time of our wedding, Paul and I wanted to start our family within the first couple of years. Ever since we were married, we had been saving money to celebrate our first anniversary. Luckily I found a great deal online on a cruise. In June 2003, we prepared to go on a cruise to Bermuda. I had just completed the school year as a middle school history teacher. Spring is always a busy season. The school year had been particularly stressful for me, filled with a lot of change, and by June I was ready for a relaxing vacation to commemorate our first wedding anniversary.

One morning I sat at my desk at work and noticed that my energy level had dropped to almost nothing. My arms and legs felt like lead weights, and I knew it would take a real effort to stand up and go about my daily routine. *Maybe I really do need a vacation,* I told myself. *Now that the school year is finished, maybe my body is finally surrendering to all the stress I've been feeling.*

I was certain my exhaustion was due to stress, but a haphazard thought skittered through my mind: Could I be pregnant? I'd never been pregnant, so I didn't know what pregnancy felt like, but I'd heard that pregnant women feel unusually tired in the early stage.

That evening I went to the drugstore and bought a home pregnancy-test kit even though I really didn't think I could be expecting. I told Paul what I'd bought, and he brushed me off with "Yeah, right."

I held my breath as I performed the test, then I gasped and blinked at the result. Positive! I couldn't believe it, but Paul and I were having a baby.

We hadn't planned this pregnancy, but we had both been relaxing and waiting to see what would happen if we let nature take its course. I showed Paul the indicator, and after getting over the shock, he was as thrilled as I was. Finally, a baby! The timing felt right, and we were more than ready to be parents.

I knew I ought to go to the doctor right away, but we were leaving for our cruise. Surely it wouldn't hurt to wait a week, would it? Thinking that I'd have lots of time to read on the boat, I picked up some pregnancy books at the bookstore. As we packed, I joked about not being allowed to lift my suitcase or drink coffee on the trip. I was ready for a baby, and prepared to give up whatever I had to sacrifice to make sure our little one arrived safely.

The following day we left for our cruise, but the trip got off to a rocky start. Because Paul doesn't like to arrive anyplace too early, we arrived only thirty minutes before our flight was to depart—but that was too late for us to be allowed to board the plane. Since we missed our flight, the airline put us on standby. We honestly thought we were going to miss the boat—literally. Three different flights to New York came and went, and finally we were allowed on a plane. We arrived in New York just in time to board our beautiful ship.

Once we found our stateroom, I lay back on the bed and thought that life couldn't get any better. I loved my husband, I loved being on a brand-new cruise ship, and I loved being pregnant. Most of all, I loved the idea of welcoming a baby into our family. My parents would be so excited!

We headed to Bermuda, and Paul and I enjoyed the fabulous ship, the food, and the entertainment. When we docked in Bermuda, Paul thought it would be a great idea to rent one of those mopeds that tourists use to explore the island independently. With the sun on my arms and the wind blowing through my hair, I rode behind Paul and felt relaxed and happy.

After riding a short while, I began to feel dizzy and light-headed.

My feelings of energy and joy drained away, leaving me weak and slightly nauseous.

I tapped on Paul's shoulder and leaned toward his ear. "We need to stop. I feel light-headed and I think I'm getting sick."

I sensed—I *feared*—that I might be having a miscarriage, but thought it more likely I was coming down with the flu. After all, I'd never been pregnant, so I didn't know what a miscarriage felt like.

Paul pulled over, and we found a public restroom. I got off the moped and went into a stall. I thought—*hoped*—I might be experiencing something like morning sickness, but when I looked down, I saw blood. Not a lot, just a slight spotting, but enough to make my heart sink in my chest.

Shaken, I went out and told Paul that we needed to head back to the ship immediately. We took our moped back to the facility where we'd rented it. I felt so weak I could barely put one foot in front of the other. I leaned on Paul and he practically carried me back to the ship. The bleeding continued, so in our stateroom I pulled out my pregnancy books and began to read, hoping to find an answer or some encouraging news.

The bleeding got heavier as the hours passed, and by sunset I realized I was losing the baby. In one of the books I read, *If you are experiencing a miscarriage, nothing can be done to prevent it.*

Nothing.

With a broken heart I realized that pursuing medical treatment on the ship or on the island would not save my baby, not at this early stage. So I spent the rest of the day in bed, sleeping, crying, and blowing my nose. Paul ordered room service for me, but I could barely eat.

I didn't go down to dinner that night, but the next day I forced myself to leave the stateroom and mingle with people. We met some fun couples at our dinner table, but I didn't say a word about what had just happened to me. I hadn't told anyone but my mother that I was pregnant, and after the cruise, I was glad I'd kept silent. Even though I'd read that many first pregnancies end in miscarriage, I couldn't help feeling a sense of failure.

I wanted to know why it had happened . . . and if I could have done something to prevent it.

When we got back home, I went to my ob-gyn and told him what had happened. He assured me that anywhere from 15 to 25 percent of all known pregnancies end in miscarriage, and most miscarriages occur during the first thirteen weeks of pregnancy. I've read that between 30 and 50 percent of pregnancies end in miscarriage before women even realize they are pregnant; they assume the blood flow is their regular menstrual period, perhaps off by a few days.[1] Yet knowing those things didn't make me feel much better. I had been so ready to be a mother.

But I would have to wait.

℮℧

Within a year, I found myself pregnant again. After taking the home pregnancy test, I went to the doctor right away. He confirmed my pregnancy and gave me all the necessary prenatal vitamins and information. Once again, Paul and I were thrilled. We had high hopes that this pregnancy would succeed—after all, the highest rate of miscarriage applied to *first* pregnancies, and this would be our second.[2]

I was working two jobs at the time—teaching during the week and selling clothing on weekends. I had a big holiday fashion show scheduled right after my doctor's appointment, and at the conclusion of the show I went to the restroom and saw that I was spotting again.

And I knew. I just knew.

After a moment of despair, I panicked. This couldn't be happening again. I had been so careful to do everything right. I was losing this second baby, and I couldn't do anything to stop it . . . could I? I left the restroom and sat down, waiting for Paul to get back from helping load boxes of clothing into the car. When I heard his voice, I found him with my mother, who was helping us pack up.

In a broken voice, I told them I needed to go to the hospital. The situation was completely different this time—we were in the United States, near home, and close to a hospital—but that same weak, helpless feeling began to overwhelm me.

Mom took me to the hospital while Paul finished packing up items from the show. He then joined us at the hospital, where a technician put me on the examination table and did an ultrasound.

Paul leaned forward and peered at the grainy image on the screen. "I see a baby . . . but it's hard to tell."

But he didn't. All the wishful thinking in the world wouldn't restore that baby to my womb.

The technicians tested the expelled tissue, and later I learned that the nine-week baby, a little girl, appeared perfectly healthy. Yet no one could give me a reason for the miscarriage.

I left the hospital feeling the same sense of failure I'd known after the first miscarriage. I didn't know why I was losing healthy babies, but I wanted to identify the problem so I could get it fixed. I never wanted to experience another miscarriage.

I didn't carry the burden of disappointment alone. Paul was also saddened by our miscarriages—each pregnancy had buoyed our hopes and made us enthusiastic about becoming parents, but the miscarriages cruelly dashed those dreams. Though Paul put on a brave face around me, my mom told me that he once broke down and cried with her. The loss of a baby is hard to handle, whether you're a man or a woman. Especially after the second pregnancy, which had lasted longer and seemed to be going well, Paul and I were left upset and painfully disappointed.

And after numerous tests, my doctor still could not give me a definitive reason for my inability to successfully carry a child to term. As difficult as it was, I had to accept that for some reason I couldn't grasp, God didn't think the time was right for me to have children. At that point in my life, it was the most difficult realization I'd ever had to accept.

Chapter Three

Playing God?

Not long after my second miscarriage, I was working at my computer and talking to a friend on the phone. Paul was in another room; we had settled in for a quiet night at home, yet another night without the sounds of children to keep us company.

As my friend and I talked, the topic of my miscarriages came up. She knew about my most recent miscarriage, and she was sympathetic because she'd had her own fertility problems. After commiserating with me she said, "I think you should go see one of the specialists I used."

"But he's a fertility specialist," I answered. "And we're not infertile."

"But he's a reproductive expert. Who knows? He may be able to help you figure out why you're having these miscarriages."

Because she had been successful in getting pregnant, I figured it wouldn't hurt to call the doctor's office and make an appointment.

So though I didn't think of myself as infertile—hadn't I been pregnant twice?—I made an appointment at the clinic she recommended. I had routine blood work done, and had a hysterosalpingogram—a procedure in which dye is injected into the Fallopian tubes and an X-ray is performed while the dye is "clamped" inside.

My reproductive endocrinologist (fertility doctor) referred me to a hematologist. A nurse for the hematologist slid a needle into my vein and filled a seemingly endless number of vials. The hematologist thought I might have a clotting disorder, but I'd never noticed anything unusual when I cut myself. He mentioned that one of his patients who had had seven miscarriages was diagnosed with a slight clotting disorder. She'd had three children since beginning treatment for the condition.

His recommendation for me? To self-administer daily shots of Lovenox, a blood thinner. He explained that one of the side effects of Lovenox is bruising to the abdomen. After taking it a few days, my belly would look as though I had suffered several bad falls.

As eager as I was to have a baby, I did *not* want to give myself shots in the abdomen. Needles terrify me, and the thought of purposefully sticking a needle into my own stomach left me weak-kneed. Why would any woman want to cause herself pain? I struggled to train my brain to accept the idea that it'd be okay to stab my stomach with a sharp syringe. The pain would be a sacrifice for the cause, and the final result would be worth the effort. I'd do whatever I had to do to get pregnant and maintain the pregnancy.

After all those tests and many sticks in the stomach, I was told to take a baby aspirin each morning. The aspirin, along with the Lovenox, would thin my blood and perhaps halt any further miscarriages.

I complied with every doctor's order, but still I did not conceive. I followed every piece of medical and traditional advice, trying everything an eager woman might try—I took my morning temperature, charted my ovulation, stood on my head. But still, nothing. No pregnancy.

While I waited to get pregnant, I applied my lifelong love of learning to the field of reproductive science. I was desperate to understand what had caused my miscarriages and how I could prevent one in the future. I soon discovered that I was not alone—in fact, some of my other friends were also experiencing reproductive problems. I shouldn't have been surprised, because the Centers for Disease Control reports that 7.3 million American partners—12 percent of reproductive-age couples—meet the definition of *infertile:* unable to get pregnant after trying for one year.[1]

In the summer of 2005, the phone rang. A nurse from the fertility doctor's office was on the line; she wanted to follow up with me. After exchanging a few pleasantries she asked if I might want to schedule an appointment with the doctor. She thought he may be able to help me. If it meant that I might get pregnant, I'd do anything, so I went in for a consultation.

"Your levels are borderline," the doctor told me, "so I don't think you should be doing the Lovenox." He glanced at my chart. "Since you've been trying to get pregnant for two years, you're now dealing with an infertility issue."

I shook my head. "I've been pregnant before. It's not that I *can't* get pregnant—"

"You haven't been able to get pregnant for two years," the doctor reminded me. "And that, by definition, is a fertility issue. Now we need to do some more tests, and we also need to test your husband."

I hadn't expected to hear this news. I thought my problems stemmed from an inability to carry a baby, not from an inability to conceive. I had never considered investigating assistive reproductive treatments or technologies.

If you've never been infertile, I'm not sure you can understand the agony of empty arms. Infertile women are not able to smile and say "me too" to other pregnant women; we are the ones who hang back when a coworker stops by the office with her new baby. Our smiles become fixed and polite when we are asked to look at baby pictures; if we are brave enough to attend a baby shower, we're often asked, "When are *you* going to have a baby?"

The entire *world* seems to waddle beneath a big, rounded belly when you are infertile. Every woman in my circle of friends seemed either to be pregnant or to be carrying a newborn in her arms, yet Paul and I came home each day to an empty house.

But we weren't desperate enough to try something as radical as artificial insemination or in vitro fertilization. Yet.

௦

As the days passed, Paul and I considered the possibilities before us. We are both strong believers in God and in the sanctity of unborn life. Before we could consider other reproductive choices, we needed to think about what they meant in terms of our faith. Would God bless us if we proceeded in this direction, or would we be making a serious mistake? Would we be "playing God" or simply taking advantage of God-given medical technology?

We weren't concerned with the question of when life begins. Paul and I agreed that common sense tells us the egg and sperm are alive before they ever unite. Life is a gift passed from the mother and father, from the grandparents, from the ancestors, and ultimately, from God. What begins at the moment of conception is a new *person*.

Paul and I knew we had to honor God's gift of life. Whatever we did, however we proceeded, we would not think of embryos as mere clusters of cells, but as our babies. They were precious to us and to God, so we knew we had to be careful in how we allowed them to be handled.

So I read articles, I looked up information from the Centers for Disease Control and the Society of Assisted Reproductive Technology, I talked to friends who had experienced some kind of fertility treatments.

My doctor decided to put me on a fertility drug for three months. They would monitor me during that time, and they hoped I would conceive while I was taking the drug.

Unfortunately, the three months came to a close without a positive result. Each month that passed without a pregnancy only reminded us of our failure to conceive.

After the three-month test, my doctor presented us with several other options. "We could do artificial insemination," he explained, "or in vitro fertilization. And, of course, you and Paul have a five percent chance of getting pregnant on your own."

Artificial insemination, the "turkey baster" approach, frightened us because at the time of insemination, no one can control or predict how many drug-stimulated eggs will be traveling down the Fallopian tubes and available for fertilization. I didn't think I'd mind twins—they run in our family—but I did not want to find myself pregnant with a half-dozen babies. The risk to mother and babies is much greater in a pregnancy with multiples. Some women with multiple embryos practice "selective reduction" and cull the weaker embryos, but Paul and I could never purposefully kill one of our babies. We knew we could never agree to eliminate any living embryo before *or* after the transfer to my uterus.

In vitro fertilization, on the other hand, sounded better to us. In an in vitro procedure, the woman receives an injection of hormones to stimulate her ovaries so they release more than the usual one egg per month. The husband's sperm is then obtained and placed in a petri dish with several eggs harvested from the mother. The hope, of course, is that most of the eggs will be fertilized. After a brief period—one, three, or five days, depending upon the clinic's philosophy—the physician will take a certain number of fertilized eggs (embryos) and transfer them into the woman's uterus. If all goes well, they will implant and the woman will become pregnant.[2]

We were concerned about inadvertently destroying life, but in vitro seemed like an ethical solution. After all, when I talked to my doctor I was told that any embryos that weren't immediately transferred could be frozen, so we wouldn't be destroying living embryos.

We had other questions. The number of eggs retrieved from each woman varies greatly, so what if I had a large amount of eggs and they were all fertilized? The doctor assured me that the extra embryos would be frozen. What if we got to transfer day and we had five or six healthy embryos? We couldn't possibly transfer that many! I was assured they could be frozen as well. From our previous experience with miscarriages, we knew that although several embryos might be created, a few would fail to thrive and grow. We went into the process knowing that some embryos wouldn't develop past the zygote stage (a fertilized ovum with two complete sets of chromosomes). We could even get to transfer day and find that we didn't have any viable embryos.

Our hope was to get pregnant with one baby. On the surface, in vitro seemed like a program we could pursue with a clear conscience.

Yet though in vitro fertilization appealed to me, the program would cost about ten thousand dollars. I blinked when the doctor told me the amount. The doctor then told me about a particular in vitro program. Women who met its health qualifications could participate at a discounted rate. The program offered hope for much less, but the cost was still thousands of dollars. He might as well have said fifty thousand.

I'm the first to take advantage of a bargain, but even so, the thousands of dollars required seemed like an exorbitant amount. Women get pregnant every day for free and I had already been pregnant twice; it didn't feel fair to me to need to spend so much money. We didn't think we'd be wise to put that much debt on our credit card, and we couldn't write a check or pay cash. Though we knew some people who'd had success with in vitro, the cost seemed way beyond our means, especially since the program offered no guarantees.

I thanked the doctor for his time and went home to talk to Paul. Because we'd been pregnant before, we still weren't convinced we were infertile. And why in the world would we spend that kind of money with no guarantee of success when every day other people got pregnant without paying a penny? We discussed the possibility of in vitro versus artificial insemination, and after weighing the risks, I thought that between those two choices, in vitro would be the better technology for us as long as no living embryos were discarded.

Paul wasn't convinced we should do in vitro. He still thought we could conceive on our own. To him, thousands of dollars seemed like too much money, and he was in no rush to have a family. I could see his point. Since we'd just bought a house, we'd either have to save money again or go into debt. So we decided to wait for a while.

But I decided to begin to save money just in case we'd need it for future fertility treatments. I sold things on eBay, mostly favor boxes for weddings and parties. I cut expenses wherever possible, we stopped eating out, and we decided not to take vacations away from home. No more cruises, at least for a while. Dollar by dollar, we invested in our future family, working hard and praying that somehow we'd be able to save enough to continue with our dreams—though I hoped that we could put that money toward a kitchen remodel instead of using it for in vitro.

One afternoon I had an encounter that changed my perspective. After work one day, I sat down with a college friend who was expecting. I wasn't jealous of pregnant women—though attending baby showers was an overly emotional experience for me, so often I simply sent a gift—but it was difficult to hide my yearning for a baby when I was around my expectant friends.

I knew my friend had been married for several years before getting pregnant, but I'd always thought she wanted to wait awhile before having children. We began to share our fertility stories, and at that moment, I knew. I became convinced that I should give in vitro a try. I was thirty-five, soon to be thirty-six, and she was the second friend I knew who owed her pregnancy to in vitro. She was a living, breathing in vitro fertilization success story, and I was certain the procedure could be the answer that Paul and I had been seeking. Why were we waiting?

In my typical decisive fashion, I went home and convinced Paul that we should try to get in on the program. Paul was hesitant to spend the money, and he still thought we could get pregnant on our own. "But I'm thirty-five," I reminded him, "and my eggs aren't getting any younger."

Somehow I persuaded him to take the next step. In December 2005, I called the clinic, but my heart sank when I heard the program was concluding. Though I couldn't be part of the program, the doctor agreed to let me go through in vitro for the same discounted rate he'd quoted me earlier. Eager to begin, I made an appointment.

In February 2006, I began the process by taking the medication that would stimulate my ovaries to release multiple eggs in a single cycle. I scheduled several appointments at the fertility clinic, cherishing the hope that *this* would be the month we conceived. But after a few tests, the doctor explained that the conditions weren't yet ideal—my body hadn't responded to the fertility drug as they'd hoped it would.

I swallowed my disappointment and agreed to repeat the procedure in March. I'd have to go back for more blood tests and the shot to super-charge my ovaries. More appointments, more pricks, more needles.

But I'd go through whatever the doctor required if it meant having a baby.

ॐ

As the blustery winds of March roared around us, Paul and I prepared to start another round of preparation for in vitro. For three weeks I took the shots, I had blood drawn, I went in for ultrasounds, I crossed out days on the calendar. And then we waited.

On April 3, I went to the clinic for egg retrieval. They put me on a table, slid an IV into my vein, and gave me pain medication. In another room, Paul donated sperm to the cause, and after extracting several eggs while I was under anesthesia, the doctors used petri dishes as a nest in which eggs and sperm could unite. Of the nineteen or twenty eggs they retrieved, sixteen successfully fertilized. Those sixteen embryos split once and officially became zygotes.

Paul and I believed that while God is the ultimate creator of life, he has given mankind the gifts of intellect and insight, allowing us to develop technology that enriches human lives. I was a little awed to think that embryos could develop in a petri dish and be successfully stored for future use.

I had emphatically stated that I wanted any extra embryos frozen for a future pregnancy. Since I could never carry sixteen babies, the doctors told me they would freeze six embryos and watch ten. I was truly concerned about how many should be watched and how many frozen—I didn't know a lot about this part of the process. I asked the nurse, "Isn't ten a lot to watch? Shouldn't we freeze more?"

"Ten is a great number to watch," she assured me. "Many of them won't survive."

I realized at that point that for all the questions I'd asked, for all the reading I'd done, I still had not quite grasped all the issues surrounding the care of fertilized eggs and the decision making during this process. From my research, I knew several wouldn't make it to transfer, but ten still seemed like a lot to watch. What if we got to transfer day and we had four or five healthy embryos? From my understanding, these embryos could still be frozen, but the doctor had said that embryos frozen early have a better chance of survival.

The clinic technicians watched ten in the lab, and their goal was to have a couple of good embryos at the end of the growth period. Depending upon the egg's genetic quality, some embryos develop faster than others, and some die within two or three days. What happens during the growth period? Through my research I learned that the cells in the zygote begin to split as the embryo develops. An embryo should be at two to four cells forty-eight hours after egg retrieval and should be at seven to ten cells by seventy-two hours.[3]

Parts of the cells may break off and separate from the portion of the cell containing the nucleus—this is called fragmentation. Though it doesn't always mean that an embryo will not result in a successful pregnancy, I read that embryos with more than 25 percent fragmentation have "low implantation potential."[4]

This particular clinic rated embryos' progress after three days, and then again after five days. I've since learned that there's controversy among labs about how long to watch embryos—some think implantation should occur after the third day; some recommend waiting until after the fifth day.

Neither do clinics agree on how to grade embryos, or what those grades mean in terms of producing a healthy child. "The true genetic potential of the embryo to continue normal development," wrote one doctor, "is impossible to measure accurately with current technology."[5]

The doctor continued, "Patients often ask whether embryos that were given a 'low grade' by the embryologist would result in a problem with the baby. As far as we know, the children born from low-grade embryos are just as cute, intelligent, strong, etc., as those born from high-grade embryos. The only difference seems to be with the chance for the embryo(s) to result in a pregnancy."[6]

Later I learned that those who favor early implantation point out that normal embryos implanted after three days have double the chance (60 to 70 percent) of producing a live birth. If embryos are allowed to grow for five or six days, those with chromosomal abnormalities will be evident and can be culled. Experts believe that those who fail to thrive within that time frame would almost certainly fail to implant.[7]

These details were not presented to us, however; we were told that some embryos would develop better than others and would therefore be better candidates for transfer. Our doctor was an expert and far more knowledgeable than we were, so we trusted him.

We wouldn't know how many embryos we had until five days had passed. At that point, Paul and I would have to discuss how many we would transfer into my uterus—we didn't want to do selective reduction later, but neither did we think we were up to the challenge of quintuplets!

Paul and I wanted to maximize our chances without maximizing our children, so four seemed too many. Triplets would terrify us, but we could handle them, with a lot of work—but we'd prefer to transfer two, because one embryo could split and you'd still end up with triplets.

I tried to consider my friends' experiences. One friend had four embryos transferred and ended up pregnant with twins. Another had three transferred and only one survived. Another had one transferred and didn't become pregnant. Another had three transferred and all three survived, but she found herself under pressure to have selective reduction because the doctor didn't think she could safely carry all three without risking all the babies. Now she regrets her choice and feels she was given poor medical advice. But when you're in the midst of that situation, it's hard to think clearly. You're in a fragile state, you're desperate for the treatment to work, and you trust the doctor who is dispensing advice. Plus for most women the goal isn't to have multiples; it's to have one baby.

As our window of time narrowed, we knew we had to make a choice. We didn't know how many embryos we'd have on transfer day, so I asked the doctor again to clarify if he could freeze any we didn't use. He told me yes, they could do that, but he reminded me that embryos frozen after they've split might not have as great a chance of survival. We understood the risks, I assured him. We just didn't want to discard them.

On April 8, marked on my calendar as "Transfer Day," Paul and I went to the office with hopeful hearts. A nurse prepped me for the procedure, which involved putting on a hospital gown and cap, climbing on a gurney, and refraining from emptying my bladder. Apparently having a full bladder makes it easier for the doctor to see the uterus, so in my enthusiasm I held my urine until I thought I was ready to explode.

Eager and expectant, I lay on the gurney with my feet in the stirrups and shivered in the air-conditioning. (Why do they keep medical rooms so cold?) The doctor came in and said we had three embryos with potential. Two of them were "really good." The third didn't look as good, so he was recommending we transfer two.

I asked if he'd freeze the third embryo, and he said yes, he would—if it was still viable.

I didn't ask him to clarify that statement—if the third embryo had been viable at the time of transfer, surely it would still be viable when we had finished the procedure—and I felt comfortable with our decision, knowing that our third embryo would be cryopreserved and waiting for us.

I lay there, awake, shivering, and uncomfortable, as the doctor transferred two embryos. I knew Paul and I could handle twins or even triplets, if one of the embryos twinned in the next few days.

Still, Paul and I thought we'd achieved real success—two embryos transferred and seven frozen for the future. We'd done all we could to turn our dreams of a family into reality.

⁀

And so we waited. And we prayed that everything would go well and I would soon become—and remain—pregnant.

One of my friends told me that I should eat a lot of pineapple because it was supposed to help with implantation. I probably ate an entire pineapple that weekend. We had invested a lot of time and money in the procedure, so if I'd heard that eating liver would increase the chance of implantation, I would have held my nose and gulped the stuff down.

As I lay in bed each night, my hands would move protectively to that place over my belly where two small embryos lived. I didn't understand the process that caused some embryos to implant and others simply to fade away, but I prayed that these two little lives would do whatever was necessary to grow and thrive in my uterus. Paul and I would do everything we could to protect them.

We went to visit friends in New York. I felt bloated and thought it was from all the drugs I'd been prescribed. Ten days had passed since the transfer, and though I had an appointment with the doctor for the upcoming week, I couldn't wait. Was I pregnant? I bought a pregnancy test at the drugstore and carefully followed the instructions. Yes! I was pregnant . . . but with one or two babies? Unfortunately, the home pregnancy test couldn't answer that question.

After exhaling on a wave of relief, I held my breath and prayed that these babies—or this baby—would survive. My next challenge would be making it safely through the first trimester.

A few weeks after the embryo transfer, Paul and I went to the doctor's office for an ultrasound. As the technician slid the transducer over my abdomen, I was delighted to see and hear two tiny heartbeats—our babies! Both embryos had implanted, so we were expecting fraternal twins.

I looked at Paul and blinked back tears. I couldn't believe our prayers had finally been answered. At thirty-six, I would give birth to much-loved and much-wanted twins. Both Paul and I were overjoyed and thankful to God for these blessings. The moment we saw those two babies' strong heartbeats on the ultrasound monitor was one of the happiest of our lives.

Knowing that we had two babies was an unexpected miracle, a double blessing. We were so grateful to know that both embryos had implanted, and we were gratified to realize that no human lives had been wasted. Paul and I felt confident that we had done everything we could to enlarge our family in a positive, life-affirming way.

I pressed my hand to my abdomen and marveled at the miracle of life growing within. If all went well, my body would nurture and protect these two little lives. My heart had already bonded to these little miracles; I looked forward to the coming months of pregnancy and the experience of childbirth.

After all the negative pregnancy tests and two miscarriages, the positive experience was beyond our expectations. After so many months of discouragement and despair, Paul and I were delighted to know that two little babies were on their way to our arms.

Before I left the ultrasound room, I asked the nurse if any of the remaining embryos had been viable enough to be frozen. After all, the doctor had said I had three with "good potential" at the time of transfer . . .

She glanced at my chart. "I'm sorry, no."

"Oh." Confused, I lowered my gaze. What had happened? Had the third good embryo died or degraded during my transfer procedure?

I might have considered the matter further, but Paul was beaming and I had two living babies in my belly. After so much grief and disappointment, we were finally setting out on the road to parenthood. God had blessed us beyond our expectations.

My happiness, however, was guarded. I couldn't forget that I'd had two miscarriages. Since I never knew what had caused me to lose those other babies, I didn't want to do anything that might endanger these precious children.

Chapter Four

Pregnant!

Several weeks passed. Though I smiled more broadly than usual, perhaps, I didn't want to tell anyone I was pregnant. I did tell my parents and my sister, but Paul and I didn't make a public announcement. The wounds from our previous losses were too raw, and I wasn't sure I could bear publicly exposing my grief. Though I appreciate compassion and kindness, it's often easier to shove pain to the back of your mind if you are not constantly reminded by the sympathy of others.

During the eleventh week of my pregnancy, one morning I went to the bathroom . . . and saw blood. I panicked. Paul kept telling me to calm down, but once you've had a miscarriage, it's hard to remain unruffled when you see evidence of bleeding. Did this mean I was losing our twins?

I called the doctor's office immediately and made an appointment for that day. The technician did an ultrasound, and I was so nervous I didn't want to even look at the monitor. I had been feeling fine, except for being tired and having headaches. As I lay on the table I closed my eyes and braced myself for horrible news. I was expecting to hear a hesitation followed by *I'm sorry, they're dead*, but instead I heard the technician say, "Here's a heartbeat . . . and here's another. They're fine."

I opened my eyes and stared at the screen, wanting to imprint the image on my brain. Yes—I could see them. Two heartbeats, two babies, both alive and well. I slumped in relief and felt a weight of worry roll off my shoulders.

"It looks like you've got a little bleed in there," the technician continued. "It'll stop eventually."

The bleeding did stop, but I was never completely at ease during my pregnancy. After a miscarriage, I don't think a woman ever completely relaxes. I refused to do amniocentesis because the procedure carries a slight risk of miscarriage. Even though I would have liked to know that my babies were okay, I would never terminate a pregnancy if they weren't. So I would be risking miscarriage for no reason.

As the months went by, I tried to follow Paul's example and relax. That summer I sat down more than usual, I put my feet up, and I did my best to rest and savor the simple wonder of having two babies growing inside me. I found myself doing things right for their sakes. I ate nutritious foods, I avoided caffeine, and I tried to avoid stress. Fortunately, summer vacation made all those things easier, and those warm months were among the happiest of my life. To my surprise, I found that I loved being pregnant. My friends kept telling me it wasn't fair; I didn't even have morning sickness in those early months, though I did suffer from migraine head-aches.

After summer break, I went back to teaching at our local middle school. By this time I was feeling pressure on my abdomen because one of the babies had settled into a head-down position. It hurt to walk very far, but still I managed to teach.

Yet the later months of pregnancy were anything but easy. Sometimes I'd experience subtle cramping and end up in the emer-gency room. On my first trip to the hospital, the attending phy-sician decided that I had gone into preterm labor at twenty-eight weeks. I had dilated three centimeters and was at risk of premature delivery, so he said I would have to stop working. He gave me mag-nesium to stop the contractions, then admitted me to the hospital for the next four days.

On my third trip to triage, the doctor admitted me and I re-mained in bed for two and a half weeks—long enough to go a little crazy with boredom. Thankfully, the hospital had wireless Internet, and my laptop helped me feel a little less isolated. I kept asking Paul to bring me books from home, and I chafed at the restrictions of movement because I was attached to so many monitors. Getting out of bed to use the restroom was more work than I care to remember.

Finally the doctor said I could go home . . . as long as I promised to stay off my feet. I called Paul the morning I got the good news and told him I was being released. He said he'd be by to pick me up around four, when he finished work.

"That's eight more hours. I can't wait that long! Please, come pick me up *now*," I told him, my voice firm. "I've got to get out of this place."

On the drive home, I lowered the window and drank in big gulps of fresh air. It felt wonderful to be free of that bed and all those wires and machines. The trees gleamed gold and orange, the falling leaves were dancing in the wind, the world practically shimmered with beauty. I have never appreciated the freedom to freely move about as much as I did in those moments.

I would have to rest in bed, and Paul would have to wait on me hand and foot, but at least the babies and I would be home, where we belonged.

℘

On November 29, 2006, Paul's oldest brother, Rod, came over to help us floor our attic. Paul, who is self-employed as a field engineer (someone who works on equipment like wind generators, AC/DC motors, control systems, dynamometers, and other things I don't understand), had to go finish a project at an automotive manufacturer, so Rod stepped up to fill in as my helper. He drove me to my doctor's appointment, let me out, and waited for me to go inside for a quick checkup. Like a good patient I stepped into the office and let a nurse take my blood pressure. But as I was leaving, the nurse stopped me. "Your pressure was a little elevated," she said, "so the doctor will want us to do an enzyme test." She handed me a paper cup, and I knew what to do with it.

I stepped into the restroom and followed procedure, then handed the urine specimen to the nurse and went outside to meet Rod.

At home, I had just settled on the couch when the phone rang. Fortunately, it was within reach.

"The doctor wants to deliver you today," the nurse told me. "Your enzyme levels are up, so you have preeclampsia. Don't eat or drink anything, because it's time."

Time to have my babies? Already?

I couldn't believe it. Though I was eager to deliver, I was only in my thirty-sixth week. I thought I'd have more time to savor this experience and prepare our home for the girls. I was aiming for a December delivery, not a November birth. "Are you kidding?"

"I'm not kidding," the nurse replied. "Just get to the hospital as soon as you can."

Because I have a phobia about knives and being cut, I was a little anxious about the Cesarean section my doctor recommended. I always thought I'd go into labor when the time was right, not when a nurse called to tell me the time had come.

But I trusted my doctor, so I hung up the phone and struggled to pull myself off the couch. I wish the nurse had told me that my situation wasn't an emergency, because I could feel panic welling beneath my breastbone. I tried to call Paul, but couldn't get ahold of him. I called my dad, though, and by that time I was gasping when I told him I was going to have the babies . . . *today.*

After about thirty minutes and multiple phone calls, I finally reached Paul. I told him the doctor wanted to deliver the twins, and he said, "Okay, I'll be there as soon as I finish up here." I rolled my eyes—that relaxed attitude is *so* Paul.

As calm and collected as usual, Paul came home, grabbed my suitcase, and drove me to the hospital. After our arrival, the staff went over details with me, rattling off more information than I could absorb in my state of panic. Their instructions went in one ear and out the other because I kept thinking about the impending operation and all the things I hadn't finished at the house. The bassinets weren't set up, we'd left dishes in the sink, and I hadn't done half the things I wanted to do before the babies' arrival.

No matter. A nurse put me in a wheelchair and took me to a birthing room, where I was propped up in a bed and hooked to all kinds of monitors. In the meantime, my parents arrived at the hospital.

Paul looked at his watch and announced that he was hungry. I wasn't allowed to eat because of the approaching surgery, and the doctor assured me that he wouldn't begin my C-section until at least eight o'clock because I'd eaten something for lunch.

"In that case," Paul said, apparently unwilling to participate in a sympathy fast, "I'm going to get something to eat." So he went off to a pizza place while I stayed in the birthing suite and thought about pepperoni and scalpels and all the unfinished tasks waiting at home.

The doctor came in at seven thirty, dressed in surgical scrubs and ready to deliver me, but Paul still hadn't returned from dinner.

I called him on his cell phone and told him to come back, but we all had to wait for what seemed like an eternity. Finally my levelheaded husband arrived. The doctor wheeled me down the hall, doubtless ready to get my surgery finished so he could go home. Nurses transferred me to a gurney and installed drapes around me. The anesthetist administered the anesthesia, and I remember shivering in the operating room. Paul stood by my side, holding my hand, trying to calm my shaking body as he peered over a drape at whatever they were doing to my belly. Something sharp pricked my skin; I heard someone on the surgical team talk about taking another job while someone else chatted about a new condo. I experienced a moment of nausea, then felt pressure on my belly.

A moment later I saw Ellie. A nurse held her up for me to see, then whisked her away to do the necessary testing. Megan followed soon after, and even if I hadn't seen her, I'd have known she was as beautiful as her sister from the ear-to-ear grin on Paul's face. The little babies that had been cocooned inside me were now out in the world, and Paul was thrilled to be their daddy.

Paul held Ellie after she'd been swaddled. Once Megan was ready, they wanted to give both babies to me, but my blood pressure had dropped and I had absolutely no strength in my arms. But knowing those little girls were alive and squalling made everything all right.

Paul was as excited as I've ever seen him. He was still grinning when he went out to meet our parents, and the grandparents were eager to hold the girls and help give them their first baths. The twins' birth became a huge family event, and I was so grateful to have my family nearby. They were thrilled to share in the excitement as soon as the babies were born.

Later, propped in a hospital bed, I smiled at my babies and then looked at Paul. Together, we'd done it. Both of us, working as a team, had managed to pool our energies and unite our efforts to conceive and deliver two beautiful little girls.

I spent four days in the hospital recovering from surgery and getting to know my babies. Then it was time for our twice-as-large family to go home.

After we buckled the babies into the car seats, Paul and I got into the front. He gripped the steering wheel and looked at me. "Do we have everything we need at home?"

I nodded. "Now's a great time to ask," I teased. "We do, but nothing is set up. You weren't in any hurry to get things done, remember?" I smiled at my always laid-back husband and caught sight of a new look in his eyes. Was it eagerness or anxiety? Or maybe I was seeing his newfound sense of responsibility for the tiny little lives now entrusted to our care. Whatever it was, I liked it. Our eyes met and a new bond of mutual dependency seemed to flow between us. Whatever we were about to face, I knew we would face it together.

After we got home, I took care of the girls while Paul rushed around setting up bassinets. At one point he tried to help me prepare formula for the girls' bottles. He mixed the liquid, poured it into bottles, and nestled Megan in the crook of his arm. With the baby secure, he popped a nipple on the bottle, then picked it up and dumped four ounces of warm formula on her . . . because he hadn't screwed the top on completely.

Not a great start, but a funny one.

In the days following the twins' birth, I often wished we could store up our sleep as easily as we freeze and store vegetables. When I was on bed rest, people use to tell me, "Rest up now because you're going to need your rest when the babies arrive." As the days passed, I learned why parents of newborns—especially when there are twins—are so often exhausted.

But Paul and I wouldn't have had it any other way.

⌒

While I was getting to know our daughters in the hospital, a woman had come in one evening to test our babies' hearing. "This is a simple test," she told me. "We're going to put these sticky sensors on their heads, and we'll be able to tell if they're hearing the signals."

I was still worn out from surgery and trying to keep two babies calm, but everything was peaceful when the woman came in. I was a little less than happy with the prospect of a hearing test, mainly because I feared she'd wake the babies when she attached the sensors to their heads. Though Megan woke and cried a little bit, she passed her test with no problems. I expected Ellie to do the same.

My luck didn't hold. The woman had a hard time getting the sensors positioned correctly on Ellie's head, and for some reason the test didn't work for her. Ellie woke up and started to cry in earnest, which only irritated me and made the test more difficult. "We'll try again tomorrow," the woman told me, giving up. "Don't worry about a thing."

The next day a different woman came in to test Ellie's hearing, and this woman seemed a little more patient. But once again Ellie didn't pass the test.

"I wouldn't worry," the woman assured me as she packed up her equipment. "This is a sensitive test, and often babies that can hear fail the exam. Ellie's a month early, and premature infants frequently fail. Just be sure to have her hearing tested in two or three weeks."

By this time I was a little concerned—any new mother would be—but not particularly worried. Deafness doesn't run in our family, and no one from our gene pool has experienced any hearing loss apart from that normally associated with advancing age.

Before Ellie was a month old, Paul and I took the girls to a local audiologist for additional testing. The technicians took Ellie into an exam room and gave her sugar water to keep her happy. I watched, fascinated, as they sent electrical stimuli to her brain to see how it responded.

"How do you know whether or not she can hear?" I asked.

The technician tried to explain the mechanics, but only one fact stuck with me: Ellie didn't pass the test. The audiologist told us she responded only to extremely loud sounds. I asked if my little girl was deaf, but the woman never gave me an absolute answer.

The audiologist flushed as she sat down to talk with Paul and me.

She suggested that we contact an otolaryngologist. She didn't say Ellie was deaf; she only gave us a referral.

That's when I began to worry. "This is just one test," I said, thinking aloud. Not only was Ellie a preemie, but she was also a C-section baby, so she could have fluid in her ears. "Could her hearing change in time?"

"It might," the woman hedged. "And it might not."

So we made an appointment with an otolaryngologist, an ear specialist, who conducted more tests and recommended hearing aids. Again, Ellie didn't pass her ABR (auditory brainstem response) test or her otoacoustic emissions (OAEs) test.

Once again we weren't told that Ellie was deaf; we simply received a recommendation.

I took the girls to our pediatrician for one of their regular checkups. He had received all of her testing results, so I was eager to hear his evaluation of her records. After his examination of Ellie, I asked if we should have more tests done. "Why?" Surprise flitted across his face. "All the reports indicate that she's profoundly deaf."

Profoundly deaf.

The words echoed in my head, and after a moment of shock, relief flooded through me. Finally someone found the nerve to tell me the simple truth. That was the first day I heard those words. None of the experts had been willing to tell us the truth: all tests indicated that Ellie was profoundly deaf in both ears.

We were devastated to learn that one of our children had been born with a birth defect that would affect her throughout her life. It didn't seem fair. Paul and I had experienced the gift of hearing every day of our lives, but Ellie had never heard our voices in the womb, never heard our words of love and concern for her. We wanted Ellie to have the same opportunities Megan would have.

From that point I went into problem-solving mode and became extremely proactive. We had Ellie fitted with hearing aids as a temporary solution, then I carried her from specialist to specialist, from doctor to doctor.

We desperately wanted to find out why she was deaf, so we arranged for CAT scans, MRIs, and genetic testing. Ellie had a perfectly shaped cochlea and her auditory nerve functioned, but though sound would enter her ear, very little sound reached her brain. No one could tell us why.

No matter what the cause of her deafness, medicine had provided a fix: a cochlear implant. A cochlear implant is a small electronic device consisting of two pieces: one piece sits behind the ear like a hearing aid, and the second piece rests beneath the patient's skin. When the microphone picks up sound, it sends signals to the transmitter and converts them into electric impulses, which are then sent to the auditory nerve.[1]

I'd read enough about cochlear devices to know that the earlier they were implanted, the easier the patient would transition from a world of silence to a world of sound. I knew Ellie would be a good candidate for a cochlear implant, but when should it be done? And how?

I called someone at the University of Michigan's cochlear rehabilitation program. I took Ellie for testing; I met with another audiologist. All the experts told me that nothing could be done until Ellie was a year old, but for my daughter's sake I was itching to get started.

Until that all-important first birthday arrived, we did whatever we could to stimulate Ellie's auditory nerves and introduce her to spoken speech. Our little girl was fitted for hearing aids and ear molds at two months of age. By three months, we had enrolled her in Michigan's Early On program and the Intermediate School District program.

After careful research, we decided that she would have her surgery at the Mott Children's Hospital in the University of Michigan Health System. Over one hundred cochlear implant surgeries are performed at that facility each year, and they have an excellent auditory-verbal-therapy program. All the while, we tried to figure out how we were going to pay for Ellie's medical treatments, implants, speech therapy, and follow-up training. We were fortunate—my health insurance would cover the surgery, but only part of the subsequent therapy. Ellie would need speech therapy until her speech and language reached the appropriate age level.

So we prayed. Since our girls' arrival, I've tried to remember to thank God for the blessings we experience every day. Despite Ellie's deafness, we had our beautiful twins, our precious daughters. Many families are challenged with medical conditions that are far more severe than the one we faced.

の

By the time November 2007 arrived, bringing with it the twins' first birthday, we were more than ready to proceed with Ellie's cochlear implant. She had been quite aware as a baby, but by that twelve-month milestone I had noticed a definite delay in Ellie's progress compared to Megan's. Megan babbled first, and when Ellie did babble, she didn't babble as much. She didn't like wearing her hearing aids and would take them off, put them in her mouth, and throw them around—all the things babies do with small objects. During that first year I felt as though I spent nearly every spare moment running Ellie to some kind of appointment—speech therapy, medical checkups, or hearing-aid checks at the audiologist's office. Paul and I also had to lead her through developmental exercises at home.

As we prepared for her cochlear implant, I asked the doctor about the advantage of having two implants instead of one. He assured me that one implant would be fine; in fact, some deaf people had made a point of "reserving" their other ear in case a new and better technology came along. But I had learned that if you don't stimulate the auditory nerve in some way, it will atrophy. If Ellie didn't have a second cochlear implant, we'd need to put the hearing aid back in her other ear.

Though we didn't like the idea of having to deal with hearing aids again, that was a small concern compared to our driving desire that Ellie have the same opportunities as Megan. Megan had two hearing ears, why shouldn't Ellie? Our health insurance company didn't want to pay for the second implant because the operation is expensive. But if she'd needed an eye, would they have given her only one and insisted one was "good enough"?

We approached the date of Ellie's operation with a mixture of nervousness and excitement. I was thrilled to think that within a month, after the implant's activation, Ellie would be getting good sound in her ear. But I couldn't help thinking about the risk—cochlear implants are tricky, and a slip of a scalpel could result in a nicked facial nerve and leave my little girl looking like a stroke victim for the rest of her life.

The hospital had a hotel attached, so we spent the night at the hotel with Ellie. We had planned for Megan to spend a couple of days with my parents, but my parents were insistent—they wanted to be with us. So my parents got a room in the hotel as well, and they took care of Megan while we sat in the waiting room during the operation.

Having surgery yourself is worrisome; waiting while your child has surgery is far more traumatic. While we waited, Paul and I tried to read the magazines scattered around the lounge area, but neither of us could focus on anything for very long. We drank coffee, we ate foods from vending machines, we walked around hallways and went nowhere. Paul wore a stressed expression that was far different from his usual look of unending calm. The waiting would have been almost impossible to bear, but an aide kept coming out to give us updates on the surgery.

We stayed with Ellie in recovery until she woke up, then we went with her to her room and took turns staying with her. She was groggy from the anesthetic, she couldn't understand why her head was wrapped in a huge covering, and she couldn't hear a thing because she wasn't wearing her hearing aid. The poor thing couldn't get comfortable to sleep, so we passed a long night before we took her home the next day.

After the first implant, we watched Ellie and occasionally saw her turn her head in search of a sound. Yes, she could hear with one ear, but that second of searching in order to home in on a sound might make a world of difference if she were crossing the street and listening for an oncoming car.

I knew that a child's window for speech and language development is from birth to five years old. After doing more research, I discovered that two (bilateral) implants significantly help deaf children. When kids receive implants without a significant time lapse between operations, their brains adapt more easily to sound. The longer patients wait for the second implant, the harder it is for them to adjust. The more I read, the more I became convinced that Ellie should be bilaterally implanted as soon as possible. Yes, new technology was being developed, but that technology wouldn't be available for years. Another cochlear implant simply made sense.

Our doctor settled the question once and for all when he admitted that if Ellie were his child, he'd recommend she receive two implants.

Paul and I established a new goal: two implants for Ellie. But how could we pay for the second operation if our health insurance didn't provide coverage? So we prayed that the insurance company would listen and respond favorably to our appeal.

The company that produced Ellie's first cochlear implant had a division to assist people with documentation on the benefits of bilateral implantation, so they worked with me in contacting my insurance company to appeal their decision. Our insurance reps took six months to come around, but between my calls and those of our advocates, we managed to move that particular mountain of paperwork to the right desk at the right time. My insurance company finally agreed to pay for the second operation. Our prayers had been answered.

In December 2008, Ellie had a second cochlear implant. I was far more nervous during the second surgery than during the first—I couldn't help feeling that I had a girl who was doing well with one cochlear implant, so what if they damaged a facial nerve during this second operation? Had I reached too far, asked for too much?

The surgery took far longer than the first had, and the surgical waiting room emptied out long before Paul and I heard that Ellie was on her way to recovery. When we finally spoke to the surgeon, I couldn't help asking, "What took so long?"

He tried to assure me that everything went well. Then he admitted that her facial anatomy was more complicated than usual, so the operation took longer. She seemed to have more difficulty adjusting to the second implant, so we were glad we didn't wait longer.

As we write this book Ellie, at three, plays just like her sister.

She's in a regular preschool, she has caught up with the others at her age level, and we plan to mainstream her in school. She's made amazing progress, and most people who see her have no idea that she was born profoundly deaf.

After seeing that Ellie was well-adjusted and happy, I thought we had managed to put our most difficult trials behind us.

How little I knew. . . .

Chapter Five

Frozen in Time

After seeing Ellie safely through her two surgeries, Paul and I turned to the matter of our six remaining embryos. We had always planned on giving our six cryopreserved embryos a chance at life. We didn't know if they'd survive the thawing or the transfer, but those babies have always been part of our family plans. Paul talked about our babies being "frozen in time," and every time I received the monthly bill for their cryopreservation, I imagined I was writing a check for children who were away at summer camp. Forty-seven dollars a month for six kids—what a bargain! I found it easier to think of them as being away at camp rather than frozen in a nitrogen tank.

We had the twins, and we had our other six children. They simply weren't living with us yet.

After we were convinced we had done all we could do to give Ellie and Megan the best possible start in life, we turned our attention to the six frozen embryos stored at a lab operated by our fertility clinic. Every month when I wrote that special check,

Paul and I would discuss if the time was right to expand our family.

We had been paying the monthly storage fee since April 2006, long before the twins were born. I remember once coming home from work and opening up the monthly statement from the clinic. Paul had been home all day with the girls, and he looked worn out. His hair was tousled, he hadn't had time for a shower, and I knew he had to be exhausted. I walked into the family room and smiled at the picture he made—he had both girls sitting in the baby glider, Megan in one corner and Ellie in the other. He was on his knees with a bottle in each hand, feeding both babies at once.

Laughing, I asked, "Hey, Paul, are you ready for more kids?"

He gave me a look of pure exasperation. "Yeah, let's do it right away."

After joking about it, we had a serious discussion and knew we couldn't even think about having more kids until the twins were at least two years old. With their needs, we had all we could handle. At the same time, however, we weren't getting any younger. We would need to make the decision to expand our family sooner rather than later.

Once the girls passed their second birthdays, we felt we were ready to handle another child or two—however many God chose to send us. If we arranged for an embryo transfer in the late spring or early summer, the baby would be born when the girls were three and a half, potty-trained, and easier to handle. I was especially looking forward to sharing the miracle of birth with Megan and

Ellie. They would be so excited about a baby. I could imagine their tiny hands on my tummy, feeling the baby kick, experiencing the miracle of growing life.

We didn't know what God's plan for our family would hold. We had no expectations other than an ordinary pregnancy. Our doctors had told us that, on average, only 50 percent of embryos survive a thaw, so even if none of the embryos survived, or if they didn't grow afterward, we would have been at peace knowing that we gave them a chance at life. The thought of carrying another multiple pregnancy concerned me, but no matter what happened, we were ready to accept the challenge.

As to those unsettling statistics about only half of embryos typically surviving a thaw, when we began to investigate in vitro I learned that the average client of a fertility clinic is older, and many have health issues. I was still relatively young and healthy, so I thought the percentage of surviving embryos might be higher for us.

I simply prayed that we'd have living embryos on transfer day.

I was prepared to handle whatever God sent our way, but the possibility of a single baby appealed to me. Carrying one baby had to be easier than carrying two—at least that's what my friends who had given birth to twins *and* singletons told me.

The previous year, Paul and I had discussed that 2009 would be a good time for our frozen embryo transfer. I was about to turn forty, and we didn't want to wait any longer to complete our family.

So on a blustery day in January 2009, I called and made an appointment with my fertility doctor. The appointment was no big deal—at that time the doctor would simply review my chart and draw up a plan for preparing my body and planning the best time to transfer the thawed embryos. The first available appointment I could make was February 23. I had the day off from work *and* free time—a rare coincidence, since I usually used my days off to drive Ellie to Ann Arbor for her twice-a-month speech therapy or audiology appointments.

After talking to the appointment secretary, I asked the office manager what the cost for another embryo transfer would be—and I learned the amount had increased about fifteen hundred dollars in three years. *I should have done this sooner,* I realized, then I quickly dismissed the thought. I had already saved some money, so I'd simply have to save more.

I was working and paying the bills, but we didn't have a lot for extras. We certainly didn't have enough to pay for another full-price cycle, so I asked about any special programs the clinic might be offering. . . . Was there any way at all to reduce the cost? I was told to ask the doctor.

While I was trying to figure out when we'd have enough money saved for the procedure, Paul was praying that he would be able to keep his business afloat. "I kept thinking about our bank account," he recalls, "and things were looking bad. I'd hit a dry spell with no work coming in, and I could see the writing on the wall—I was either going to have to find work or fire the babysitter. There was nothing coming down the line, no prospects in my immediate future.

"I knew how much I had and what wasn't coming in," Paul says. "Then Shannon told me about the fertility clinic and what plans had to be made. I knew she wanted me to help pay for it, but I only had enough for the babysitter and bills for two or three months, maximum. If I couldn't pay the babysitter, then I couldn't go out and get new projects to work on. It's a vicious cycle. I would have to stay home full-time until a job came up, and then where would I get the money to start my business all up again? I would probably have to go out of business.

"So as the weeks went on and the pressure escalated, I got to the point where I couldn't take any more. Finding money at that point was like squeezing blood from a stone. So I sat down in my office and quietly looked around. I began to breathe deeply. I calmed my mind and began to meditate on the situation and what to do. I knew from the past when I worked in sales that when everything looks bleak and the clock is at the eleventh hour, somehow God always finds a way, but we have to provide the willpower to trust him.

"I had no idea what I was going to do, so I simply sat there with tears in my eyes and began to pray. 'Heavenly Father, what am I doing wrong? Why are things so difficult right now? What do I have to do? How am I going to pay for all these bills and this procedure coming up? I don't know what I'm going to do—did you abandon me?

" 'You know, I don't know how I'm going to deal with this. I can't leave our babies frozen in time. Please, I don't know how to do this.'

"I didn't want our unborn children to be frozen forever, but I needed forty-five hundred dollars for the procedure, so they either had to stay frozen or . . .

"I didn't know what I was going to do. So I asked God if there was something that could be done . . . if he could give us some kind of help, no matter what way, shape, or form. We just needed an answer.

"I had so many questions, but mostly what I needed was reassurance for the future. I sat there for a long time, I don't know how long, and regained my composure. When I was finally calm, I decided to let all my problems go and just have faith and keep working. I knew we could trust God to figure it all out."

Chapter Six

The Other Woman

With my fertility appointment for February 23 circled on my calendar, I tried to focus on ordinary things—taking care of the girls, my students, and my husband. Paul and I were excited about the prospect of enlarging our family, but I knew some things couldn't be rushed.

Be patient, I told myself. *Enjoy these days with your girls. Once you bring a baby home, things will become hectic again. . . .*

But then we received a phone call from our fertility doctor, and we visited his office. And there we heard the staggering news: all our frozen embryos had been lost due to a "terrible incident" in the lab. As we sat in the doctor's office at the fertility clinic, suddenly it seemed like time stood still. For a moment the clock on the wall seemed to stop ticking as my heart and mind began to race.

Feeling slightly nauseated, I glanced at Paul, who was trying to keep one of the girls from knocking over a lamp. I thought of our hopes and all the dreams we'd invested in our frozen babies. Too shocked for words, I forced myself to focus on the doctor's purposely expressionless face.

When the doctor hesitated, I looked at Paul and he at me, but neither of us said anything. What could we say? After a moment of tragic reflection, I shook my head. "How did this happen?"

I expected to hear about a thunderstorm or some sort of electrical failure. I braced myself, preparing to mourn our loss. Our quest to enlarge our family was over. We were going to be the parents of two girls—no more, not ever.

Undoubtedly other couples had lost their embryos too. Had the doctor given this news to others as well?

"Your embryos," the doctor finally continued, "were transferred into another woman."

My stomach lurched as I fell back against the chair. Behind me, I could hear Paul warning the girls to be careful around the lamps; his attention had been distracted by our two active two-year-olds.

I leaned forward and focused on the doctor, holding his gaze and waiting for the next piece of information. I would not let him go until I had answers. "And?" I asked, not sure what I wanted to hear. "She's pregnant?"

The doctor nodded slowly. "Yes."

I let the air out of my lungs and looked away as the room began to spin. Our babies—how many?—weren't dead; at least one had settled down to grow inside another woman. A woman who wasn't his mother.

I clung to the armrest of the chair as I tried to sort through my twisting emotions. I couldn't believe what I'd just heard. A chill shivered up my spine and every muscle tensed. This couldn't be happening to me; it shouldn't happen to anyone. This clinic had protocols; they had safeguards. Hadn't they said so? I was supposed to be carrying my babies. I had an appointment scheduled for next week, for pity's sake, so what on earth had gone wrong?

No, no, no. My heart pounded to the rhythm of the word stuttering through my mind. But even in the midst of chaos, my practical nature pounced on the problem and searched for a solution. What went wrong?

"How?" I looked at the doctor again. "How did this happen?"

"We believe it was due to an error in the lab," he said, his voice softer now. "Human error."

Human error had put our embryo inside another woman. Impossible. Unbelievable. But apparently true.

And in that horrible moment, I realized I was powerless. I couldn't fix anything in this situation. Another woman was carrying our child or children, and we were all at her mercy. I could do nothing to solve the problem.

I couldn't have felt more violated.

I closed my eyes as my thoughts turned toward God: *Of all the people in the world—of all the people who have embryos at this clinic— why did this happen to us?*

The doctor sat silently, watching me—probably giving me a moment to collect myself and sort through my feelings. Words failed me as I resisted a wave of anger and another of grief, then questions began to tumble in my brain.

"How far along is she?" I asked, my voice sounding loud and shrill in my own ears. "The other woman."

The doctor must have known I'd have questions, because he was quick to answer. "She's about ten days from transfer."

"Isn't that a bit early for a pregnancy test?"

"Yes. I don't test that early, but her doctor does."

"She's not your patient?"

"No, she's not."

"Where, then? Where does she live?"

"I don't know—I believe she lives some distance away."

Our babies could be anywhere. And anything could happen to them. "So it's early, and there's a chance she might not be able to maintain this pregnancy."

The doctor nodded. "That's true, it's very early."

"Does she know? That she's pregnant with someone else's babies?"

"She knows."

My thoughts narrowed, focusing on the woman who carried our hopes and dreams. "How old is this woman?"

"Um . . . about your age, I think."

"Do you know anything about her?"

"Sorry, I don't have much information."

"Is she married?"

"Yes, and I hear they are a wonderful family."

Hearing that she was part of a wonderful family didn't mean a thing to me in that moment. A woman I'd never met was carrying our babies. I had no idea where she lived, who she was, if she was healthy, or what she would do next. She might be prone to miscarriage . . . and surely my doctor knew more than he was telling us.

"Does this woman have other children?"

"I think she has a baby. Maybe six months old or so."

"What in the world was she doing, having another baby so soon?" I asked, thinking aloud. But maybe she was older and didn't want to wait.

Immediately I put myself into her shoes. Our roles could have been reversed. I could have been the one carrying another family's child. What would I do in that situation? How would I feel? What would I tell people?

A jumble of questions piled up in my brain, so I picked one off the top.

"Does this woman—does she still have frozen embryos?"

The doctor nodded. "She does."

The other woman, whoever she was, held all the power in this situation; we had nothing, none whatsoever. We would have no input in her upcoming decision. The thought of hiring a lawyer immediately popped into my mind; could we legally prevent her from having an abortion? Of course not, she had every right to do whatever she wanted. Paul and I had no authority and no legal right to influence her decision. The clinic didn't even have to tell us her name.

Later I learned that the other woman was given options. She could continue the pregnancy and give the baby or babies to us at birth, she could stop taking her medication and experience a probable miscarriage, or she could terminate the pregnancy. She could sweep our babies out of her life and out of this world. She could terminate, wait a month or two, and then go back to the fertility clinic to try again with her own embryos.

The other woman was strongly urged to terminate. Aborting the pregnancy would have been completely legal, because neither Paul, nor I, nor our babies had any legal rights in the situation. All our embryos had been thawed, while hers remained safely frozen.

Our hopes for a future pregnancy were finished. Over. I was thirty-nine, and the eggs used for our frozen embryos had been three years fresher. My thirty-nine-year-old eggs would most likely be of poorer quality than the ones we had used in the previous cycle.

More questions sprang to my lips as I thought about our embryos. "How many of our embryos survived the thaw?"

The doctor tilted his head. "I *believe* three did . . . and those three were transferred."

Well, that's good, I told myself. Three survived the thaw, fulfilling the law of averages, and for a moment I felt relief knowing that all three had been transferred. Then I worried again—how many of those embryos would implant? How many babies would survive?

If the woman was carrying twins or triplets, the risks to her health and the babies' health just shot upward.

Surely this was a nightmare and I would wake up at any moment. . . .

"Yes, three were transferred," the doctor said. "But they didn't look so good. I never transfer such low-quality embryos."

"Three," I whispered. "Low quality. So there's a chance none of them will survive."

"That's right. It's early, so anything can happen."

I understood his unspoken implication. The woman might miscarry. If she was about my age, she was an older patient, and older women had a lower success rate. Her status as a patient at a fertility clinic indicated that she had experienced reproductive difficulties in the past. After learning that she was pregnant with another woman's babies, she might even be *hoping* to have a miscarriage.

Opposite desires tugged at me—I wanted my babies to survive, but in *another woman?*

I grimaced, imagining the stress the other woman had to be experiencing at that moment. What if the stress was too much and caused her to miscarry? Losing the pregnancy would solve her problems, but it would also mean that we'd lost all of our remaining embryos.

"How did this happen?" I asked again. "What kind of human error could result in this? I thought you had procedures in place. Weren't our embryos labeled by name and number? I thought you had different ways of checking."

"Shannon, I understand your frustration. Believe me when I say that everything that can be done is being done. We had an extensive meeting and discussed all the circumstances. The other family has been contacted, and for now we're going to wait to see if the pregnancy is viable."

His words barely sank in. "But I don't understand. How could an error of this magnitude happen?"

"I don't know, but we're going to do a complete and thorough investigation."

"How can you not know how this happened?"

A pained look crossed the doctor's face. "The other doctor told me that you have similar names. That may have been an issue."

In a flat voice, I repeated the little information I'd been given. "So, let me get this straight. . . . There was an error made in the lab. Our embryos were mistakenly thawed and transferred into another woman. She's ten days from transfer, the pregnancy is still very early, there were three embryos transferred. She's been notified that she's pregnant with someone else's child. This was human error, but you don't know how this happened. The only thing you can tell me is that we may have similar names." A sudden realization struck me. "Did they use two different last names like Paul and I?"

Paul and I had enrolled at the clinic under "Paul Morell" and "Shannon Savage," my maiden name. Though we had been married several years, I hadn't officially changed my name on my driver's license or insurance card. Since I was thirty-two when we married, I planned on keeping my name because it was simpler. Not until

August 2006, four months after our first in vitro transfer, did I legally become Shannon Savage Morell.

"Weren't both our names listed?" I asked. "Plus, there were numbers attached to our file."

"That's correct," the doctor told me. "But still, somehow, someone made a mistake. I can assure you that no one was drinking or anything like that."

Drinking? The idea of someone drinking or using drugs was the furthest thought from my mind.

"Do you know"—I drew a deep breath—"if this other woman is willing to continue the pregnancy?"

"She can't"—from the back of the room, Paul spoke up—"she can't terminate."

"Yes, she can," I reminded him. "Women have control over their own bodies."

The doctor shifted uneasily in his chair. "I don't know that answer."

"Does she have any health problems?"

"She's not my patient, so I don't know."

What do you know? I bit back my rising frustration and tried to focus on what could happen next while the doctor discussed possible outcomes with Paul and me.

The woman could terminate the pregnancy—the most likely result and our greatest fear.

She could miscarry. We would grieve if she lost the pregnancy, because a loss would mean no more babies for us. We'd have to be content with two girls. That wouldn't be difficult; we loved our girls and had no plans to expand our family by going through another in vitro cycle.

Or the woman could continue the pregnancy and become a de facto gestational carrier. Most people equate gestational carriers with surrogate mothers, but in the strict language of reproductive technology, in traditional surrogacy a surrogate mother supplies the egg that results in a baby for an infertile couple. A gestational carrier, on the other hand, is not genetically related to the child she carries.

If this woman agreed to act as our gestational carrier, could we legally claim our child after birth without a formal, written arrangement?

The doctor had no answer for us. He attempted a smile. "I understand you had an appointment with me next week."

"I did. I guess we can cancel that now. I still can't believe this. If we had met with you earlier, this might never have happened."

I glanced back at Paul, who wore a shocked expression even as he tried to keep our active girls from ransacking the doctor's office. This doctor hadn't made the mistake, but this *practice* had. My thoughts turned toward the legal ramifications.

I caught my doctor's eye. "Do you need to report this to the CDC?"

He lifted a brow. "I don't know."

"Has this ever happened before?"

"Not in our clinic."

But if it had, would you admit it?

I asked about the Centers for Disease Control and Prevention because I knew clinics routinely reported their success rates to the national office. Would they also report their mistakes? If other couples were considering this fertility clinic, didn't they have a right to know what had occurred here?

I shook my head. "I don't see how this could happen."

"I can assure you that we're taking pains to ensure this kind of mistake will never recur."

His answer irritated me. He had to know more than he was telling me, and didn't we deserve to know the details? How could it be fair to tell us that all our embryos had been removed from storage and transferred to another woman without explaining how such a mistake had been made?

"If she does continue with the pregnancy, how do we go about obtaining our parental rights?"

"I'm sorry, I don't know. I'll have to find out. The best-case scenario would be for her to act as a surrogate for you."

Surrogacy was something I'd never considered. If we established a surrogate/client relationship, I would probably need to pay her for her services and her medical expenses.

But Paul and I didn't have money saved up for a surrogate. Would my medical insurance pay for her prenatal care? And we'd need a lawyer to draw up papers.

It was all too much to think about.

"That would be great if she continued the pregnancy and

agreed to act as a surrogate," I answered slowly. "But how likely is that?"

A chilly silence fell between us. Finally the doctor pressed his hands together and leaned toward me. "What I need to know now is . . . what can I do for you?"

Tell us how this happened. Tell us who this pregnant woman is.

I shook my head, astounded by the blunt simplicity of his question. So many issues, but my list of important needs was a short one. "We'll want to find out who the other couple is," I told him, "and we'll want to know if they're planning on terminating the pregnancy. Then we'd like their names and numbers because we'll want to speak to them."

The doctor nodded. "I'll contact their doctor and see what I can find out for you. I hear these are nice, reasonable people who want to keep this whole matter private. When I find out more, I'll call you."

Still stunned, I nodded. "We want to keep this private too. The last thing I want is the media finding out about this. I don't want our story appearing on the local news."

The doctor agreed with me. He was probably grateful that we wanted to keep this nightmare quiet. This kind of publicity would undoubtedly affect his practice.

I gave him a tiny, strained smile. "When will we know this is a viable pregnancy? And when will we know how many embryos implanted?"

"We'll know when she has an ultrasound—and she'll probably

have one within the next two weeks. Would you like to make contact with the other couple before or after the ultrasound?"

I considered the question. I wanted to find out who the other couple was right away, but it would probably be better to wait until after the ultrasound, when we hoped to have more information. At that point, we'd know how many babies were growing . . . if any were growing at all.

So many thoughts coursed through my brain. I wanted to scream at the man, but what good would that do? Why had this happened? Why were my babies growing inside a complete stranger? Who was she, what was she like? Would she be willing to work with us, or would she make things even more difficult?

I had so many questions and no answers. But the crucial question was this: Was this woman willing to carry the baby of another couple? Or would she find the idea repugnant and decide to end the pregnancy? Was she the kind of woman who would erase the life of another mother's child? That's what we had to find out.

Paul and I quietly exchanged a few thoughts about when we should meet the other couple, then I spoke up. "We'd at least like to have their contact information—names, phone number, and where they live. We don't need to meet them in person until after the ultrasound, when we know this will be a viable pregnancy."

The doctor nodded. "I'll see what I can do for you."

"Thank you," I said, reverting to ingrained polite habits. The words fell into the space between us, sounding stupid and silly in the refined elegance of the private office. I couldn't believe I was thanking him for giving us the worst news we'd ever received. But what else could we do? We needed his help if we were going to learn anything about our absent babies. If our babies were going to live, not only would we need the cooperation of complete strangers, we could need a miracle for the pregnancy to survive.

Feeling as though I had aged ten years in the last ten minutes, I stood. Paul and I shook the doctor's hand, and he said he'd be in touch. He thanked us for coming and said he was sorry things happened the way they did. Almost as an afterthought, he added that as my doctor, he'd be willing to do whatever he had to do to help us expand our family. From his words, I inferred that he was promising a complimentary in vitro cycle if this unexpected pregnancy didn't work out.

His offer seemed inappropriate, given the circumstances, and Paul and I knew we would never visit this clinic again. We were happy with our two girls, and, given my age and the age of my eggs, we knew we'd never consider another cycle of IVF.

I stepped out the door, my mind spinning with the realization that another woman was pregnant with our child and we had no rights at all.

So many emotions whirled in my heart—terror, betrayal, and sadness. But one emotion overshadowed all the others: an appalling horror at the lab's error.

As we walked down the hallway in a stunned daze, Paul quietly said, "Why us?"

I had no answer to give him.

Paul and I bundled up our girls and stepped out into the frigid night, our hearts as chilled as the winter air.

We buckled the girls into their car seats, then climbed in and put on our seat belts. Finally, after Paul started the car and pulled out of the parking lot, I spoke the words that had been running through my mind on a continuous loop: "I don't believe this has happened. Another woman is carrying our embryos—and she could be pregnant with one, two, or three babies."

"It'll be okay," Paul said, keeping his eyes on the road. "Maybe she'll continue the pregnancy."

"How can you say that?" Torn by despair and frustration, I turned to face him. "You can't be that naive. She has all the rights in the world. Tomorrow she could walk into any abortion clinic and rid herself of this problem. We have no rights until this baby or these babies are born."

Paul kept insisting that we did have rights. I kept arguing that we didn't.

"Well, that's wrong," Paul said, and I agreed. But the laws are what they are, and the two of us were powerless to change them. All we could do was wait and pray that she wouldn't terminate.

As we made the trip home, we kept looking at each other in stunned disbelief. "Is this really happening to us?" I whispered. "Can you believe this is happening . . . to *us*?"

Paul shook his head.

"This is the kind of story you see in the *National Enquirer.* This just doesn't happen."

I found myself desperately hoping that the other woman believed in God. That she had strong pro-life views. That she would realize that she carried our family's last, best hope.

The realization of our bizarre situation fully hit Paul on the drive home. As we talked, he found himself wondering what was going to happen, what the implications would be, and how the mistake could have occurred.

"That's when the questions hit me," he told me later. "What was the other woman going to do? Keep the baby? Were things going to be okay? I knew this was our last shot at having more kids, so it wasn't like we could start over again."

I kept trying to imagine what it would be like to hear that I had another couple's baby growing inside me. I knew I could never terminate a pregnancy even if I was carrying someone else's child, but would she feel that way? Did she feel invaded? Violated?

She could legally end the pregnancy without anyone knowing what had happened. She could keep everything private. I assumed the clinic would accept responsibility for their negligence and offer her a refund . . . and I figured they'd offer to transfer her remaining embryos without charge. After such a major mistake, though, would she want to continue as their patient? I wouldn't.

I *had* to talk to her. I wanted to know everything about her. Most of all, I wanted her to know about us, to know that we were decent people who desperately loved and wanted our babies. But we didn't know who she was or where she lived. How could I convince her to continue the pregnancy? Tomorrow the doctor might call with more information. Maybe I'd soon have her name and phone number and we could talk. But what if I called and she refused to speak with me? What else could I do?

Paul and I discussed what might happen if I volunteered to act as a surrogate for her. The idea didn't seem plausible because I certainly couldn't have her embryos transferred that week; the preparation process took time. But if I did act as her surrogate, how could I handle two-year-old twins, a new baby, a late-term pregnancy, and a full-time job?

"What if we did that but I miscarried her baby and she carried mine to term?" I asked Paul. "I'd feel terrible." The more we talked about it, the more ridiculous the scenario seemed, but at that point, we were willing to do absolutely anything to save our baby or babies and help the other woman.

At that point we both became incensed about the lack of respect accorded to our embryos. We were under tremendous pressure, unbearable tension, and anxiety because someone hadn't done his job.

Our babies had been taken away from the safe place to which I'd entrusted them and then placed in the care and keeping of a nameless, faceless woman who didn't even live near us.

My heart ached in my chest as I thought about the news that only three embryos had survived the thaw. That meant three others were lost to us.

My grieving process for them began in that moment and continues to this day because later I learned that five actually survived the thawing process. Both Paul and I will think of my frozen babies for the rest of my life and wonder what they might have looked like if they'd continued to grow. What kind of personalities would they have had? I'll always wonder about the two babies I miscarried as well. Paul and I think of them as our babies in heaven, and we imagine them looking down and watching our family. They didn't have the opportunity to live on earth, but we believe we will meet them in eternity.

As a mother, I have always done everything I could to protect my kids. As we began the in vitro fertilization process Paul and I stressed that we could not discard a single embryo. We chose a professional, reputable clinic, and our doctor had been highly recommended. I asked specific, detailed questions and struggled to be a responsible parent.

Yet we had been powerless to prevent this horrible mistake.

As the full realization sank in, I felt as though someone had taken our children from a safe place and dropped them at a street corner where a stranger had kidnapped them. At any moment, the stranger could kill our babies. Her embryos were still safely cryopreserved, so why shouldn't she end this pregnancy and have her embryos transferred in a month or two? She was barely ten days pregnant, so she couldn't possibly be showing. No one but her doctor and husband would need to know what had happened. She could face her family and friends with a smile, calmly putting the past behind her.

Dear God, please let her be pro-life.

If she chose to terminate the pregnancy, we'd have to deal with our emotions about her killing our child or children.

Paul and I found ourselves at the mercy of a total stranger. Because we couldn't protect our children, God would have to protect our babies for us.

We resolved that all we could do was wait and have faith that God loved and cared about us. Paul came to that conclusion—and that place of faith—before I did. "There's a kind of faith you have to lean on," he says now, "but that kind of trust is not easy."

I've always believed in God—I grew up knowing about him and have never doubted him—and over the years I've learned that we have very little control over the things that happen to us. It's easy to say "Let go and let God," but it's hard to *live* by that credo. Yet when you're going through tough times, you have to learn how to trust that closed doors are shut because God closed them for his own good reasons. I try not to worry about things that are out of my control, and I've realized that when I can't fix something, I need to step back and let God handle the situation.

I worked hard to find some balance between what I knew in my head and what I felt in my heart. That God could be trusted, and that what had happened to my babies was beyond my control. Paul and I agreed that the only thing we could do was to put our babies in God's hands and trust that he would work things out. I think we might have gone crazy if we hadn't had a source of inner strength and faith that God always works things out for our ultimate good.

So we did all we could do—we prayed. We begged God to convince this stranger that our babies were precious and their fragile lives mattered. We prayed that she would continue to nurture this pregnancy and allow our babies to be born.

And then . . . we braced ourselves for the time of waiting.

Chapter Seven

Chasing Needles in Haystacks

Even though I had placed the final outcome of our situation in God's hands, I knew he expected Paul and me to do our part in safeguarding our family. After we arrived at home and put the girls to bed, I sat at my computer and went online to gather whatever knowledge I could find. I searched for reports about mistakes in fertility labs, and I looked up legal information to learn if we had any lawful right to the child or children the other woman was carrying. I also needed to know how surrogate arrangements worked in Michigan. I did searches for *embryo mix-up, surrogacy, surrogacy lawyers, parental rights,* and any other pertinent phrases I could think of.

I found very little, but what I found was eye-opening.

In 1998, a white woman from Staten Island gave birth to two boys: one white, one black, because an embryo from another couple had been mistakenly transferred to her. She kept both boys for several months, until a State Supreme Court awarded the black couple permanent custody of their biological son. Most horrifying to me was the fact that the embryologist *had known* that another couple's embryos had been implanted in the wrong woman, but he had said nothing.[1]

I remembered hearing about this story in the news. To think that the embryologist had known all along and said nothing! At least our clinic had told us within a few days of uncovering the mistake.

In 2004, a law firm offered a California woman a financial settlement to resolve a malpractice suit against a fertility doctor who had implanted her with the wrong embryos and hid his mistake until the baby was ten months old.[2] I gasped aloud when I realized that my doctor could have waited to see if the other woman would miscarry before telling us the truth about what had happened to our embryos.

In 2007, a couple in Britain, known only as Paul and Deborah, found themselves in our situation. They had one remaining viable embryo, but when they went to have it transferred, they were told there'd been an accident in the lab. Later they were told that another woman had received their embryo. The woman became pregnant, and, after learning that the child wasn't her genetic offspring, she had terminated the pregnancy.

Deborah later told a reporter, "I was in total shock when the hospital said it had been transplanted into another woman—not only that, she had made the decision to terminate it. It was killing my baby and possibly our last chance of becoming parents again."[3]

Her husband, coincidentally also named Paul, told a reporter: "We were in shock and very upset that such a thing could

happen. . . . When they said there had been an accident in a labo-
ratory we thought the embryo had been knocked off the table and
damaged in that way. But to lose our baby this way is unbearable
and unforgivable."[4]

The fertility clinic offered the couple free in vitro treatments,
but they refused, saying they would never go back to that hospital
because of their "torment and distress."[5]

I completely understood that couple's emotional turmoil. Ours
would only grow worse if the woman with our embryos terminated
her pregnancy. *Stop,* I told myself. *Keep thinking positive. Keep be-
lieving she will continue the pregnancy.*

A British newspaper recently reported that in vitro fertilization
is a growing industry in the UK, resulting in the birth of around
12,500 babies each year. More than 36,000 women attend the UK's
136 clinics for fertility treatment, according to the *Guardian,* and
"That's a lot of embryos in a lot of petri dishes in a lot of freezers.
You can see how the occasional mistake happens: all it would take
is a technician's moment of inattention, the phone ringing, a col-
league asking a question, and—just like that—the wrong petri dish
is plucked from the shelf and a terrible, private tragedy is set in motion."[6]

One woman's comment haunts me to this day. Linda has two
children from in vitro and strongly suspects that one of them isn't
genetically related. "I can't really explain it," she told a reporter from
the *Guardian.* "It's just an instinctive thing. He smelt different as a
baby, he looks different, he just is different. I love him—I love him

to bits—but I feel more and more that he probably isn't mine."[7] I can't help wondering—if that baby isn't Linda's, whose is it? Is there a heartbroken couple in Britain who doesn't know their child is attending the kindergarten down the street?

After our story hit the news, someone discovered that at an in vitro facility outside New Orleans, dozens of embryos were mislabeled, misplaced, and missing, forcing approximately one hundred couples to wonder if their children are their biological offspring. The clinic agreed not to accept new patients until the problem is solved.[8]

I stayed up for hours, scouring the Internet, searching for any answers I could possibly find online. Paul woke in the middle of the night and asked me to come to bed, but I couldn't. I had to feel like I was doing something, anything, to save my child. Shock still numbed my emotions, but the more I searched for help, the angrier and more upset I became. I found no answers to our dilemma; in fact, as I read about similar situations, I realized that our doctor's practice had at least admitted their egregious error. They made a monumental mistake, but at least we'd found out early in the pregnancy. Still, what could I do to save our child, to *find* our child? Nothing . . . all I could do was wait.

I finally went to bed with troubling thoughts and tossed and turned all night. When I woke up the next morning, my first conscious thought was *My child is growing inside a stranger.*

I got out of bed and felt as though I were moving in slow motion through a world that had somehow tilted; everything seemed out of balance and slightly altered. Somehow I got to work, met with my homeroom students, and took attendance. I had a preparation hour slated for first period, so as soon as the bell rang and the kids emptied my classroom, I walked down to my friend Deanna's room. I needed to talk to someone, and Deanna would understand because she'd had babies through in vitro. I knew I could confide in her and she would keep my secret.

I didn't want to spread the word, but neither did I want to bear such a burden alone. I would be sharing it with Paul, of course, but something in me wanted another woman's feedback and commiseration.

I walked into Deanna's room, closed the door, and blurted out the entire ordeal. As my words poured out, incredible relief overwhelmed me—along with a renewed sense of shock, as in the telling, the situation became more real. More concrete.

As Deanna heard the news, she gasped, put her hand over her mouth, and blinked back tears. When I finally finished, she whispered, "I can't believe that happened."

"I can't either. But it did."

Deanna and I set out to discuss my options, then we both came to the same sad realization: I really didn't have any. All Paul and I could do was wait. We still didn't know if the other woman was going to terminate the pregnancy. If she chose to continue it, I'd need to learn her name, where she lived, and how we should prepare to move ahead.

Most important, Deanna agreed, was the matter of our parental rights. Did we need a lawyer to help us establish our legal standing? Could we handle things with the clinic by ourselves, or did we need professional advice? Would the clinic help us in my efforts to contact the other woman, or would we be on our own?

I didn't have answers to any of those questions, and neither did she. After discussing several "what ifs," we agreed that, for the moment, all Paul and I could do was pray that the unknown woman would be willing to carry our embryos to term and then willingly surrender the baby or babies.

That's a lot to ask of a complete stranger.

⁊

The next days seemed to pass with unbearable slowness. I spent every available minute searching for answers online. I watched the clock and jumped at every phone call. Was it the doctor with news? Was this the call that would inform us that the unknown woman had terminated her pregnancy? Or was this the day we'd learn that she had miscarried? At this moment, were our babies alive? I couldn't bear the realization that another woman held the power of life or death over our child or children. I understood her pain, but even as I struggled to sympathize with her, my longing and concern for our babies drove me crazy.

If only I could *do* something. If I could send her a letter, I'd let her know I was willing to do whatever she asked of me, if only she were willing to continue the pregnancy. If she wanted a contract to act as our gestational carrier, we'd do it.

I tried to put the unanswerable dilemma out of my mind, but I couldn't. Some of my turmoil would ease once I knew that our baby or babies were still alive. So why wouldn't the phone ring?

After spending two days in a tangle of uncertainty, I hurried home after work and found Paul with the girls. "Did you hear anything from the doctor today?"

Paul looked at me, a hint of regret in his calm expression. "No, he didn't call."

Later that evening I went down to the basement and didn't hear the phone ring. When I came back up, I found Paul standing in the kitchen. He gave me a meaningful look. "The doctor called."

I stopped in my tracks and braced myself for bad news. "What did he have to say?"

"He said he had good news." Paul picked up the paper on which he'd scrawled a message. "The other couple," he read, "do not plan on terminating the pregnancy, and they have no desire to raise the child." His voice was thick with emotion. He raised his gaze to mine.

A wave of pure and simple relief swept over me; those were the sweetest words I'd heard in my life. This unknown couple, whoever they were, wanted to give our child or children a chance.

"Read the message again," I said, eager for reassurance.

My shoulders relaxed as relief washed over me. Our child, or children, were safe! And we were not going to have to fight over who would parent them.

As Paul and I celebrated the news of our answered prayers, I remember thinking, *The other couple must be pro-life.* We'd experienced many peaks and valleys in our in vitro experience, but this was definitely a peak.

In that moment, we decided that we'd like to make contact with the other couple as soon as possible. Instead of waiting for the results from the ultrasound, we wanted to meet them before the procedure. We wanted to thank them for their selfless act, and we wanted to let them know we were willing to cooperate in any way.

I returned my doctor's call so I could ask some other questions. In the course of the conversation, he mentioned that the other couple had scheduled an ultrasound for March 3, and the scan should reveal whether we were dealing with a single or multiple pregnancy.

I told him that we wanted to meet with the other couple before the ultrasound, if possible. He could give the other couple our phone number, our address, anything at all. We simply wanted to make contact.

He promised to talk to the other couple's doctor and said he'd call me back if he had any new information.

Hearing from the other couple, even indirectly, made me even more eager to contact them. I tried to go to work and take care of the girls as if nothing had happened, but I couldn't get thoughts of the other woman out of my head.

Oh my goodness, I realized, *she must be a basket case.* I knew all about the struggle of infertility, and I had tasted the strong desire to have a baby. The other woman must have been overjoyed to hear that she was pregnant and devastated to learn she was carrying another couple's child. This had to be the most terrible thing that had ever happened to her and her husband. All I could think was: *What can I possibly do to help make this situation better for both of our families? What can I do to ease their pain? How can I make this situation better?*

Over the next few days, I tried to go to work and take care of the girls as if nothing had happened, but I couldn't get thoughts of the other woman out of my head. I also found myself worrying about her health. Women who visit a fertility clinic tend to be older or have health complications, so we added good health to the list of things we prayed for on this woman's behalf. At that point, we had no idea how many babies she was carrying. She could be carrying triplets, twins, or just one. And so we thanked God for his intervention and we waited, eager and anxious, for the next bit of news.

Now that we knew the other woman planned to continue the pregnancy and surrender any resulting children, we searched seriously for legal help. I knew that even though the other couple had said they were going to surrender the baby at birth, they could change their minds. They could leave the country, or decide to contest our claim. I had no reason to think they would do anything unexpected, but sometimes the best-laid plans go awry.

Meanwhile, Paul was concerned about a completely different issue—what if I became pregnant during this time of waiting? The idea of some strange woman and me both having our babies around the same time felt strange—like having twins with two separate women. The same thought had crossed my mind, but I knew this was unlikely, so it didn't bother me. But it was helpful to know Paul's concerns and it reminded me that though we were both going through the same experience, each of us had unique and complex responses to it. We'd have to pull together as a couple and do all we could to understand and support each other. This was something else to pray about.

One evening, as Paul and I talked about our next steps, he looked at me. "So, do we need a lawyer now?"

I nodded. "Yes, but it can't be just any lawyer. It has to be someone who understands reproductive technology and specializes in surrogacy." I smiled at his surprised expression. "I've been researching lawyers online."

Internet searches had led me to a short list of surrogacy attorneys. But because I didn't know where the other couple lived or where the transfer had taken place, it was hard to know in which state I'd need a lawyer. I found myself hoping that the other couple didn't live in Michigan because our state law is unfavorable toward surrogacy. Although we hadn't signed a surrogacy contract, we might need one, and Michigan law doesn't honor surrogacy contracts.

I hoped the couple lived in another state. We lived only a couple of hours from the state line, so the other couple could live in Michigan, Ohio, or even Indiana.

As I talked to various lawyers, I knew I'd have to be careful about which details I divulged. Our case could potentially garner media interest, so I did not want to attract a publicity-hungry lawyer. Publicity was the last thing we wanted—our number one goal was obtaining parental rights to our child or children. We did not want the situation exploited. We needed someone who understood reproductive technology and was an accomplished surrogacy attorney. Our top priority was obtaining our parental rights while protecting our family's privacy and the privacy of the other couple.

We found Ellen Essig of Cincinnati, Ohio. Eighty percent of Ellen's practice deals with surrogacy law, so I called her. She listened to a bit of my story, then suggested that I find a lawyer in Michigan, our home state. She gave me two referrals.

The first attorney was out of town, so I left a brief message. I spoke with the second attorney, but I didn't think this attorney was a good fit. I was determined to find the right legal counsel.

Ellen followed up with me the next day. The case had intrigued her, and she felt we needed a comprehensive legal team. Paul and I agreed, and we were relieved she was interested in taking the case.

So within a week we officially engaged Ellen Essig to represent us. She educated me about surrogacy issues and pointed out that since Michigan doesn't recognize surrogacy contracts, it might be better if the other woman gave birth in Ohio, regardless of where she lived.

We weren't sure if her suggestion was feasible. After all, we still had no idea where the other couple lived. If they lived hours from Ohio, would they be willing to drive several hundred miles to deliver a baby? We didn't know, and all we could do was wait for answers.

As odd as it may sound, on some days I found myself wishing that I was the woman carrying the wrong baby. Though surrendering the child would be painful and difficult, I wanted to think those stressful months of waiting might have been easier emotionally. At least I would have known all the facts and had some control over the situation. Would it be easier, I wondered, to care for someone else's child than to spend hours wondering and worrying about the unknown? But I knew in my heart that for her, the wait must be unbearable, as she spent every waking hour carrying a child who wasn't hers, bonding with a baby she would ultimately give to us. Her pain had to be tremendous.

If I were the other woman, however, at least I would still have my cryopreserved embryos. That would be a comfort, but I'd spend months dreading the day when I'd have to say good-bye to my unexpected passenger.

And it dawned on me that this woman and I each had our own unique burden to carry. I would spend these coming months in the darkness of uncertainty, not feeling my child growing within me, not taking Paul's hand or my daughters' hands and placing them on my tummy to feel the flutters and kicks of life within. I wouldn't know what this woman was eating, or how she was caring for herself and my child. This other woman, on the other hand, would be making decisions every day to care for her body and the tiny life within—a pregnancy she sought and pursued at great personal cost, but the life within, genetically, would never be her child. It would always belong to another family.

Those tense months, I realize now, were the most difficult Paul and I had ever endured together.

⟳

Family has always been *the* top priority for both Paul and me. Paul says that he looks at me sometimes and thinks that my childhood was "Norman Rockwell-ish." My family celebrates the holidays with lots of traditions, and we like everything to be festive and happy.

"For my family," Paul says, "Christmas wasn't always a happy time. I've always felt a void, like pieces missing, when it comes to family—maybe it's because my father died when I was young. I'm sure Shannon thought I was being negative during those first couple of years when we were going out, but then she experienced one of our family Christmases. Our family is like, 'Okay, let's eat. Okay, let's open gifts. Okay, let's watch TV.' Not a lot of drama going on in our house growing up, but Shannon's family spends hours opening gifts, raving about what the gift is and how much time must have been spent shopping for it. Christmas is an all-day affair for them, but it's rarely been like that in my family.

"But Ellie and Megan have changed that for me. I have made a new beginning with them. I see the excitement in their eyes and the smiles on their faces, all from the simplest things. They always have fun, even when they should be getting to bed or cleaning up after themselves. Since they've come into the family, they've brought a goodness and spirit that seems to fill the air. It doesn't matter what the occasion is, they make it seem like it's the only thing taking place in the world.

"Until we had the girls, I don't think I ever had experiences like this. Their happiness makes me happy, and even though I didn't have the same kind of childhood they're having, being able to make them happy makes it all okay for me."

Though Paul's childhood was less than perfect, mine was special. I am still close to my parents, and we visit them so often that I think I could point our van in the direction of their house and the vehicle would automatically know the way.

My grandparents were also an active part of my childhood. Our hometown was so small that we didn't get a McDonald's until I was eight years old. Despite the appeal of skinny burgers, my mom usually cooked at home, so the only time I got to enjoy McDonald's was when we'd drive to Toledo to visit my paternal grandparents.

My grandmother Marva loved McDonald's and introduced me and my sister to Happy Meals, which soon became our hands-down favorite meal. Grandma Marva would take us to the drive-through, then she'd park her orange Pinto in the parking lot while we sat in the car devouring burgers and fries.

I learned a lot from my grandmother. My sister and I would spend a week with her every summer until the time I started working. As sharp as a pin, she was vitally interested in current events and politics, and she read Ann Landers every morning. Though we agreed on many things, we would get into spirited debates over political and social issues. She modeled a positive outlook on life.

My daughter Ellie reminds me of Grandma Marva. Their builds and personalities are similar, and whenever Ellie frustrates me, I'll smile and say, "Okay, Marva." Grandma was the kind of woman who always saw the glass as half full. Whenever she was confronted with a difficult situation, she'd say, "No problem" or "No big deal."

While I was away at college, Grandma would send me boxes of homemade chocolate-chip cookies. If I was in class when the care package arrived, my girlfriends would inform me that I had a box waiting back at the dorm . . . because they knew I'd be handing out homemade cookies later in the day. Marva also sent newspaper clippings, cartoons, and newsy letters.

She died five days before my wedding. I still miss her.

I was also close to my maternal grandmother, Isabell, who passed away in March 2009. Though I wouldn't consider Isabell a feminist, she was a modern woman who believed in self-reliance and hard work. She was one of the most determined women I've ever met, and she was an example and inspiration to my sister and me.

Grandma Isabell lived through the Great Depression, so she knew how to stretch a dollar. On one of her senior bus trips, the tour group stopped at a casino, where everyone in the group was given a ten-dollar roll of quarters. After spending a couple of hours in the casino, the group climbed back on the bus. The tour guide jokingly asked if anyone still had his or her ten-dollar roll of quarters, and Grandma Isabell was the only one who raised her hand. Life had taught her to save, not to gamble.

She entered the field of education and taught third grade for many years. I remember visiting her classroom as a young child, and it may have been those visits that inspired me to become a teacher myself. In her later years Grandma Isabell was always proud to announce that all three of her granddaughters had earned their master's degrees and worked in education. She met former students wherever she went, and their enthusiastic greetings and gratitude always inspired me. I hope to influence just as many students' lives.

Grandma Isabell always loved people, and people enjoyed spending time with her. I've never met a woman with a busier social calendar. I loved her very much and confided in her, so I knew I had to talk with her about the horrible clinic mistake as soon as I could, before she left us.

Grandma had been battling congestive heart failure for many years, and at the end of January 2009, her doctor admitted her to a hospice unit. Paul and I took the girls to see her every weekend, and on the weekend following our horrific news, I sat by her bed and poured out my heart. I wasn't ready to tell the world or even my parents about our situation—so far, Deanna was the only person I'd told. But Grandma had always been a good listener and a great confidante.

Isabell embraced modern technology and was one of the few people who knew Megan and Ellie had been conceived through in vitro. She loved being the first to know of the possibility of impending birth. I knew that if the unknown woman's pregnancy continued, Isabell probably wouldn't live to see the birth of her third great-grandchild.

So I sat beside her and told her the story of what had happened to our frozen embryos. Through her pain, Grandma listened and nodded, her eyes filling with sympathetic tears as I shared our heartbreak and anguish. I told her we could do nothing until the baby was born, and I asked her to keep our secret.

Grandma nodded as her hand found and squeezed mine.

I'll never forget the wistful look in her eyes. If the pregnancy continued successfully, it would result in the birth of a great-grandchild she would never see . . . at least not on this earth. But I found comfort in thinking that maybe she and Grandpa would look down on us from the balconies of heaven.

ᶜ

While we were visiting Grandma on that Saturday afternoon, we received a phone call from my doctor. He gave us part of what we'd been waiting for: the name of a contact—a lawyer—for the other couple. I could barely breathe as I grabbed a piece of paper and wrote down the number, recognizing the area code for Toledo. Maybe they lived in Ohio—that would be great news! Now we had a second piece to the puzzle.

I called Ellen and left a message with the contact information, and later she called and said she would speak to the other attorney on Monday.

I did some quick Internet research and learned that our contact practiced law in Toledo. Because most people would try to find an attorney close to home, I thought it likely that the other couple lived in Ohio as well. This was good news for us. Though, as Ellen pointed out, we lived in Michigan and had hired an Ohio attorney. . . .

I called Ellen and left a message with the contact information, and later she responded that she would call the other attorney on Monday.

Slowly but surely, we were moving forward . . . toward what, we still didn't know.

Paul and I spent a lot of time playing detective in an effort to identify the other couple. We knew that someone in our contact's law firm had gone to school with the unidentified husband, so we began a search for some kind of connection. The fruitless exercise was like searching for a needle in a haystack, of course, but at least it gave us something to do.

Chasing needles in haystacks was more fulfilling than sitting and doing nothing.

Chapter Eight

Talk to Me, I'm Listening

On February 23, I looked at the notation on my calendar and steadily crossed through the reminder of my doctor's appointment. If I had legally changed my name from Savage to Morell right after we got married, perhaps this entire situation would have been avoided. Or if I had scheduled my appointment earlier . . . That appointment had been canceled, of course, since we no longer had any embryos to transfer. This should have been a happy day, filled with expectations and dreams for the future as we took a step to expand our family. Yet instead of reporting to my doctor, Paul and I performed another significant act that day: we signed documents to officially hire Ellen Essig to represent us.

The next day we received an e-mail from Ellen. She had been in contact with the other couple's attorney. The only information the lawyer shared was the news that her clients were still very emotional about the situation. The wife was thirty-nine, and the couple had another child who was approximately six months old. They lived in

Ohio, and, after consultation with their religious adviser, they had decided not to abort the pregnancy.

Ellen and the other attorney agreed to talk again in two weeks and left open the possibility of a future meeting of their clients with both attorneys present. Our contact said her clients were not ready to share their identities, but hoped that everyone concerned would be willing to keep the matter private. Ellen shared that privacy was also one of our goals.

Later I asked Ellen what would happen if the other couple *never* released their identity. Could they have our baby and simply fade away?

"In that case, we'd try to get a court order," Ellen told me. "But let's not worry about that yet."

I accepted her assurance, but I did want to meet the couple who had our child. I thought they'd want to meet us and know whose baby they were carrying. Wouldn't it be logical for us to work through this situation together?

"The wife is too distraught and upset," Ellen explained. "So they're not ready for a meeting at this time."

This news didn't make me happy, but the other woman's feelings were easy to understand. After all, if she lost the pregnancy the problem would disappear and her life would never have to be tangled up in ours.

I knew I might feel the same way if the situation were reversed. This woman, whoever she was, had spent the previous month enduring shots, numerous blood draws, and ultrasounds. She had gone through the embryo transfer procedure, then she had waited and probably prayed that those precious embryos would implant. About ten days after the embryos had been transferred, she went in for the routine pregnancy test. As the hours went by, she waited for the phone call every woman longs to hear: "You're pregnant!"

She'd had a positive pregnancy test and she had rejoiced with her husband, grateful that all her hard work had resulted in success.

Then she'd been told that someone made a mistake . . . and the baby in her womb wasn't hers, but someone else's. The joy she'd been savoring must have drained away, leaving her feeling invaded and abused. Her dream of another baby had turned into an infertility nightmare. She had to be asking why this happened to her family . . .

Paul and I felt terrible for her. The situation wasn't fair—not to her, not to us. Yes, I wanted to know who she was for reasons that had to do with protecting and connecting with my child, but I also wanted to reach out to her. After all, I'd been through in vitro too. I had lost precious babies before, and in this fiasco, had lost my precious embryos. We had both fallen victim to the clinic's error and I wanted to make a connection.

I thought that if the four of us—Paul and I, the woman and her husband—could sit down together, we could work as a team to find a solution and help one another navigate this unbelievable circumstance.

A few days later I visited my gynecologist for my regular well-woman checkup. As I sat on the table and answered the routine questions, he glanced at my chart. "What about those frozen embryos?" he asked. "Are you and your husband ready to expand your family?"

I took a deep breath. "It's funny you should ask. I just found out that they've been transferred into another woman." Trusting in doctor-patient confidentiality, I shared the little information I knew. He shook his head and murmured something about being appalled by the lab's negligence, but he hoped everything would work out for us. "Let me know if there's anything I can do for you," he added.

I thought that dismal, gray winter would never end. The gloom of socked-in skies and long nights only added to the darkness of our emotional turmoil. I searched the sky for days, hoping for a glimpse of sunshine, proof that summer was on its way. Each day that passed I knew that my baby, or babies, were growing inside a woman I did not know. I ached with the desire to be carrying this child—the last of my offspring—within my own body.

February faded into March, and at the beginning of the month I received a call from Ellen. The other couple's lawyer had called my attorney with an update. She had received a call from the husband, Ellen explained, and the wife had had an ultrasound. The pregnancy was progressing well.

"That's great," I answered, my heart racing with joyful relief. "How many babies are there?"

Paul and I had been discussing a lot of "what if" scenarios. We were prepared for another set of twins or even triplets. Though our house already felt too small with the four of us, we had agreed that no matter how many embryos survived, we would welcome them with open arms.

"Just one baby," Ellen said. "One baby with a good heartbeat, and the due date is October 29."

I released a long sigh. Thank goodness there was only one baby. Carrying one baby would present a lower risk of health problems for our child and the woman carrying him or her. We would have welcomed multiples, but given the circumstances, we felt blessed knowing at least one baby had survived. But still, an unexpected sense of loss nudged at me. My other embryos were gone forever. This child would be my last.

"What about the woman's health?" I asked Ellen. "Is she going to be okay?"

Ellen assured us that the woman was well. I exhaled in relief. So far, so good. Paul and I were cautiously optimistic. At this point, it looked as though we had one baby. But I knew we'd be on pins and needles every time we received an update, afraid the ultrasound would reveal no heartbeat at all.

The next day I sorted through the mail and found an envelope from the fertility clinic: the monthly bill for the storage of our frozen embryos. I know the invoice was probably a computer error, but that paper felt like a sick joke, a sad reminder that we no longer had any embryos in storage.

On Saturday my fertility doctor called to ask if we'd heard any news from the other couple. I told him we had, and he shared that the woman's doctor had confirmed one pregnancy with a healthy heartbeat. As if to reassure me, he added that the other doctor had told him the other couple were "wonderful people."

My doctor asked if there was anything he could do for us. I told him I'd just received another bill for the frozen embryos, so could he please ask his billing office to stop sending us invoices?

"I will take care of it," he promised.

He asked if we had drawn up any paperwork yet, and I said, "Not yet—the other couple hasn't revealed their identities, but they seem willing to give us medical updates."

He asked if we'd engaged someone to represent us, and I assured him that we had. Then he mentioned that he'd like me to come into the office at our convenience for additional testing. I murmured a noncommittal answer and hung up, knowing it might be the last time I would speak with my doctor.

Our lawyer had advised us to stop all communication with the doctor and the clinic. The clinic kept calling and asking me to come in for blood work and tests, but I thought they might be trying to cover their liability—I couldn't see the point of all those lab tests. If my embryo posed some sort of physical risk to the other woman, the damage had already been done. Testing me for AIDS or other sexually transmitted diseases seemed pointless, as my embryo had been created three years earlier.

I discussed the matter with Ellen, and she advised me to refuse any further testing. Frankly, at that point I'd been given so little information that I didn't want to hand over my complete medical history. I knew nothing about the other woman, so why weren't they advising me to have *her* tested for AIDS? After all, she was carrying our child and could theoretically put the baby at risk.

Once the other couple revealed themselves and opened up communication, I would be willing to have whatever testing they requested. Until that time, I could see no reason to release any medical information.

.℮◯

One week slowly stretched to two, then three. We were growing weary of living in the limbo of uncertainty. For weeks Paul and I prayed for the other couple without knowing who they were. I tolerated that lack of knowledge. After all, I understood they needed time to adjust to the peculiar reality of the situation we shared. We prayed too for the growing baby. For weeks our only communication came through lawyers, forcing Paul and me to interpret e-mails filled with lawyer-speak.

Every day I would focus on what the other woman was experiencing. What was she thinking? How was she feeling? She and her husband probably thought they were doing everything they could by giving us updates, but we really wanted a personal connection. They wanted to protect their privacy, and I understood that inclination, but it was hard to wait and be told, "This is how we're going to do it."

One afternoon I glanced at my computer and saw that I'd received an e-mail from Ellen. Attached to the message was the first scanned photo of our growing baby. I glanced at it, then looked at Paul. "Want to see a photo of your child?"

Paul stopped in his tracks. "What do you mean?"

"A picture of our baby."

"How'd you get a picture?"

"From Ellen. Look." I turned the computer so Paul could see the image. "There's our little Peanut."

Paul shot me a quizzical look. "Our what?"

I laughed. "The pregnancy book says that a baby is about the size of a peanut at nine weeks."

The name stuck. Because we knew the pregnancy was still precarious, we were careful about what we said around the girls, occasionally mentioning our hopes for Peanut's continued growth. We used the pregnancy book to follow along with the other woman's progress. She was nine weeks along . . . with thirty-one weeks stretching ahead.

After several weeks, I told my lawyer that Paul and I wanted to send the couple a letter. They didn't have to respond; we simply wanted them to know how much we appreciated what they were doing for us. If I were carrying another couple's baby, I'd want to know a little about the other family.

Ellen agreed to pass the letter to the other attorney, who would convey it to the other couple. So I poured out all the feelings in my heart:

Hello!

First of all, my husband and I would like to express our appreciation and gratitude that you decided to continue the pregnancy. We both realize it would have been easier on you to terminate the pregnancy. This entire situation for us has been extremely stressful. We were relieved the pregnancy wasn't terminated. This was our first concern. I was also relieved there was just one baby. I carried twins and know the stress it can put on a woman's body.

My name is Shannon, 39, and my husband is Paul, 38. We live in Michigan. We have two daughters, Ellie and Megan, born November 2006.

We understand the grief and pain that accompany infertility. I had two miscarriages before giving birth in 2006. After the miscarriages, we experienced infertility. After other unsuccessful treatments, we spent many months saving money to undergo in vitro.

Paul and I always planned on more children. We've felt blessed with two girls, but we were always planning on thawing the six embryos . . . I was shocked to find out that our embryos had been thawed and transferred into another woman. Then we were told that she had a positive pregnancy test. We were stunned. We couldn't believe a mistake like this could happen. We were told that the person didn't follow proper procedure. I questioned this again and again. The doctor said we had similar last names. I couldn't believe this, as there would have been two last names filed. At the time of the first in vitro procedure, my legal name was my maiden name. I hadn't changed it to my husband's last name.

I immediately reflected that I could have been the woman who had a stranger's embryos. I've spent a great deal of time thinking about this.

We've felt powerless since the beginning. We were told that three embryos survived the thawing, but they didn't look good. We were thrilled to learn one had survived. Though I wonder . . . if I had all three transferred, would more than one have survived? It's still early in the pregnancy. Though I pray the pregnancy will be successful, I realize it may not be. So again, I think, "what if?" For me, those frozen embryos were my last chance at attempting a pregnancy. I was looking forward to this experience and sharing it with my girls.

Paul and I have kept this matter private. Our family has no idea what has happened. My maternal grandmother is in hospice care right now, and my family doesn't need further stress. On another note, Paul and I weren't open about our infertility, nor do people know that my girls were in vitro babies. Besides a few close friends, my parents, and my sister, no one knows. I really didn't want to share my medical history with other people.

. . . It's unfortunate that this had to happen. This is hardly an ideal situation for either of us.

For right now, I try to think about the positive side of this . . . God, for some reason, decided that another woman would carry this baby for me. We hope you'll be willing to share this experience with us. We'd like to learn more about you, and we'd like you to know more about us.

Thank you for the prompt updates. We spend a lot of time waiting and wondering. We'd appreciate any information you're willing to share.

Thank you for continuing the pregnancy and treating it as if it were your own. I understand the tremendous stress you must be under, and we pray it will be successful and, in the end, a positive experience for you. Then we certainly hope you'll be able to thaw your embryos and once again have another pregnancy.

> *Shannon and Paul*

After we sent the letter, we waited for a response . . . and waited some more. Because the other woman was still in the early stages of pregnancy, she could still miscarry . . . and if she did, she and her husband would probably want to quietly continue their in vitro quest without further contact with us. I understood why they didn't want us to know their names or where they lived. But at the same time, not knowing who was caring for our baby amplified my feelings of being left out of my baby's life at a time when Paul and I should have been enjoying that unequaled experience of harboring our own flesh and blood growing within my body.

Meanwhile, another major stress was creating pressure for us. My grandmother Isabell's health was failing. She was slowly slipping away from us, and I dreaded the thought of losing her. We traveled several hours north to see her every Sunday, and each week

I could see signs of her steady decline. Her breathing grew shorter, her smile weaker. The girls understood that Grandma wasn't feeling well, but every visit reinforced my certainty that death was imminent.

We were awaiting the birth of a child as we watched another loved one fade away. Death and birth . . . two bookends in the progression of life, both momentous and emotional.

Paul and I both had a hard time coping with all the stress, so we focused our energies on the girls, work, and home. One of my coping mechanisms was simply avoiding the subjects of pregnancy and loss. If I didn't talk about them, I could get through my daily tasks. As long as my mind was occupied with other things, I was able to function almost normally.

On the drive to and from work, however, and when the house was quiet, that's when I couldn't help thinking about our baby. Those first two and a half months were painfully slow and long. My grandmother was dying before my eyes while a faceless woman was carrying my child. Watching Grandma Isabell's rapid decline made me think far too much about death. Would my baby survive this horrible situation?

In late March, I called Ellen to see if she'd heard anything new. "No," she said, explaining that we were in a kind of lull.

I thanked her and hung up, dissatisfied and frustrated. I knew we were in a lull, and I was impatient to be out of it.

Later that day, however, an e-mail arrived telling us a bit more about the other couple. We had asked for their names and a few details about their family, so Ellen relayed a message from their lawyer:

At this time my clients are able to provide your clients with the following information:

1. They are approximating that they live no more than 100 miles from your clients.

2. They do have living children who are in perfect health and have experienced normal development from birth.

Attached please find an ultrasound picture taken on Monday, March 23, 2009. The baby measured nine weeks, one day at the time of the ultrasound, which is indicative of healthy fetal development. The heartbeat at the time of the ultrasound was 180 beats per minute, which is very healthy as well. This is promising progress.

Eagerly we clicked on the image and studied our unborn child. I thought back to the first ultrasound of our twins, remembering how my heart had leaped at the sound of their beating hearts. I wondered what emotions this woman felt when she heard the heartbeat. Did she smile? Or did she cry because the beating heart was not that of her own baby?

We still didn't know the other couple's name, but at least we knew they had healthy children and lived only two hours away. That meant a drive to meet them wouldn't be out of the question . . .

when they were ready. We'd been given only a morsel of information, but to Paul and me, it seemed like a feast.

After a few moments of elation, however, I felt the sharp stab of disappointment. That was it . . . all they could tell us for now. We were in store for a long eight months.

On March 28, my beloved grandmother died, taking my secret with her. Two days later I attended her funeral, where I gave a eulogy in which I spoke about what I'd someday tell my children about their grandmother. She lived a full life, without regret, and died ready to go home.

I only wish I'd been ready to let her go.

⌒

I was eating lunch in my classroom when Abigail, one of my co-workers, popped in. She sat down at a desk and began to eat her lunch. "Guess what?" she said. "I have some news."

I looked up, suspecting what I was about to hear.

She must have seen the suspicion in my eyes, because she laughed. "That's right, I'm pregnant."

I gave her a sincere smile. "Really! Well, congratulations. When are you due?"

"November 6, I think."

"That's really great." I kept my face calm, but behind the mask I was playing mental Ping-Pong. Should I tell her my news? Yes or no? I hadn't planned on sharing the announcement with anyone else, but suddenly I had to spill the beans.

"Guess what? I'm pregnant too."

"No way!" Her eyes glowed. "Congratulations. When are you due?"

"October 29."

"Wow—we're going to have our babies at practically the same time."

"Yes . . . but I'm not having our baby."

Her smile twisted. "What do you mean?"

I took a deep breath and launched into my explanation. Few people knew that Megan and Ellie had been conceived through in vitro, so first I had to explain that, and then tell her about the frozen embryos, and describe how we'd been anxious to try for one last pregnancy . . . until we learned that our embryos had been placed inside another woman's uterus.

"And she's pregnant," I finished.

Abbey stared at me, her mouth open. "I can't believe it."

"I couldn't either—at first."

I now had two friends who knew my secret. Two friends, one husband, one lawyer, and one grandma—who was now gone. I'd managed to hide the truth from everyone else.

Another day I was standing in the hallway when another teacher came by and mentioned that I looked stressed. I wanted to tell her I had a good reason to be stressed, but instead I talked about the frustration of preparing our income taxes.

One evening, in an effort to work through my feelings with God, I wrote in my journal:

Dear God:

I have many questions only you can answer.

Could I not have another successful pregnancy? What do you want us to learn from this? I have a lot of questions. Have you been giving me answers? Am I not listening? Is there something else you want to tell me? You've got my attention. What is it I'm supposed to do?

This experience has filled me with every possible emotion.

You've got my attention, so now what? What's the next step in this journey? You've got a plan, I know it.

Talk to me. I'm listening.

Shannon

I think I hid my extra load pretty well, because no one else seemed to notice. Their unawareness of our situation kept them from asking questions and extending sympathy, and in our situation, at least, their ignorance resulted in our bliss. We found it easier to behave normally when no one knew our secret.

After learning about Abigail's pregnancy, I knew she would be a daily reminder that another woman was pregnant with my child. She was about a week behind the woman carrying our baby, and we were about the same height. She would be like a mirror, so as I watched her pregnancy develop I'd be able to imagine what the other woman looked like as she carried our child.

One afternoon I pulled Abigail aside and mentioned that I had a few maternity clothes she might be interested in borrowing. She

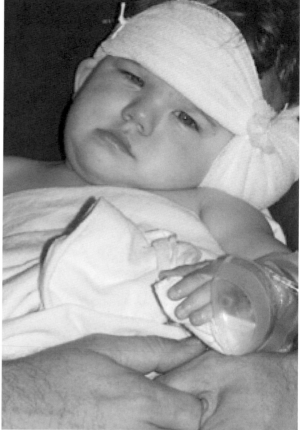

Right: Ellie recovering after her first cochlear implant surgery, December 2007; below: Paul with Ellie in the hospital, December 2007

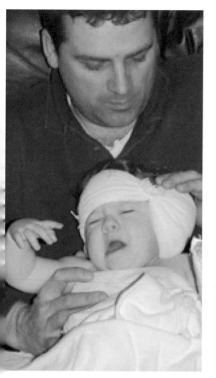

Shannon and the girls with Grandma Isabell, Christmas 2008

Paul and Shannon with the girls, April 2008. *Photograph by Stephanie TeSlaa.*

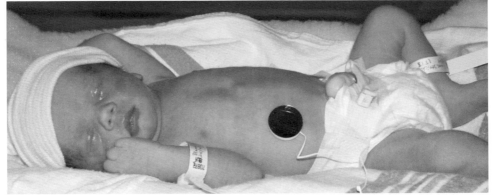
Logan under the warmer at the hospital, as the doctor tries to raise his body temperature, September 2009

Paul holding Logan within hours of his birth,
September 24, 2009

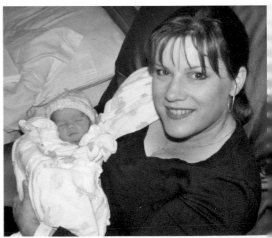
Shannon holding baby Logan, September 25, 2009

In Carolyn's room after the Savages spent an hour alone with the baby, September 25, 2009

Megan very excited to be holding Logan for the first time, September 25, 2009

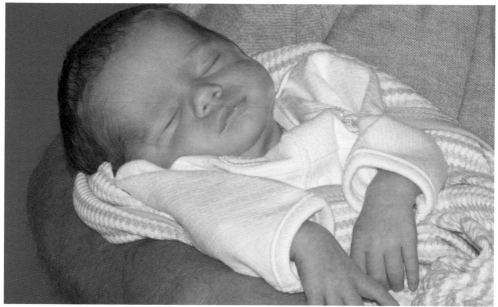

Grandpa John holding Logan (just two days old)

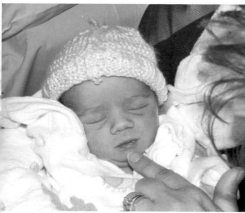

Looking at the new little miracle

Shannon bringing Logan home

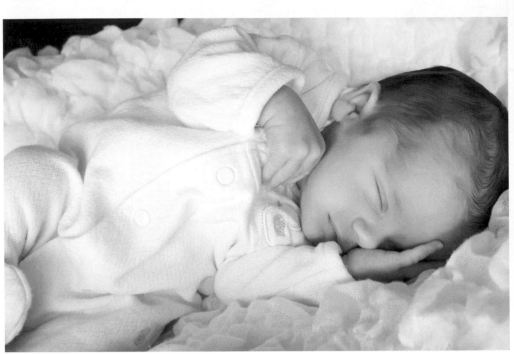

Logan sleeping, October 2009. *Photograph by Stephanie TeSlaa.*

The Morell family ten days after Logan's birth. *Photograph by Stephanie TeSlaa.*

The girls with their baby brother.
Photograph by Lisabeth Conger.

Logan (one month old). *Photograph by Lisabeth Conger.*

Logan ready to start his morning
(about four months old)

Shannon, Ellie, and Logan.
Photograph by Lisabeth Conger.

Top left: Megan the bunny holding Logan the pumpkin, Halloween 2009; top right: Christmas; middle left: Little Christmas gift *Photograph by Lisabeth Conger*; middle right: Megan kissing her stocking stuffer, November 2009 *Photograph by Lisabeth Conger*; bottom: Shannon and the kids celebrating her fortieth birthday

Mom and Dad kissing Logan February 2010. *Photograph by Stephanie TeSlaa.*

Left: Happy
Logan *Photograph
by Stephanie TeSlaa;*
right: Logan
*Photograph by
Stephanie TeSlaa.*

Logan laughing.
*Photograph by
Stephanie TeSlaa.*

The Morell family. *Photograph by Stephanie TeSlaa.*

Loving on Logan. *Photograph by Stephanie TeSlaa.*

was grateful, so I asked Paul to go up into the attic to bring down some clothes. He came back with a few boxes.

I thought I'd be able to happily loan those clothes to my friend, but the act of touching those garments took me back a few years, and for the first time I bowed my head in heart-wrenching regret. I began to cry as I lifted out my maternity tops, and memories came flooding back. Even though my last pregnancy had been somewhat difficult toward the end, I had adored the feeling of life growing inside me. I had enjoyed the experience of being pregnant.

I had carefully packed these clothes away, knowing that I wanted to wear them for one last pregnancy. The realization that I would never be pregnant again felt so final . . . almost as if I had agreed to have a hysterectomy or had unexpectedly found myself in the midst of menopause.

No more babies. I was finished with childbearing.

In that moment, a surge of emptiness hit me with the force of a blow and I shed the first tears I'd wept since learning about the fate of our stored embryos. We'd been cheated. Though Paul and I were expecting a child, we were missing out on the entire experience. We would never feel our child move beneath my skin or see his little hands flutter in my belly. We wouldn't feel the first kick, experience his hiccups, or collapse from the exhaustion only pregnancy can bring. I would never be able to show my girls a bulging belly and explain that Mama was carrying their little brother or sister inside her.

It wasn't right, nor was it fair. I wanted to go outside and scream; I should be wearing these maternity clothes.

But no matter how badly I wanted to rant and wail, I knew that somewhere not too far away a woman was doing all the things I wanted to do and feeling sad because she'd miss out on midnight feedings, the first tooth, the first step, and the first date. I would miss out on a few months of growth; she would willingly walk away from *years*.

With those thoughts in mind, I knew I could deal with whatever I had to bear.

Chapter Nine

The Meeting

On April 1, the other couple's attorney sent us another e-mail update with an attached ultrasound picture provided by the couple. In this photo, Peanut measured at ten weeks and three days. His or her heart rate was a strong 184 beats per minute. Everything pointed to continued healthy development, and the attorney's unnamed client would have another appointment on April 8. The lawyer would forward the results from that appointment as soon as she received them.

Paul and I were thrilled that the other couple was prompt with updates and e-mails, even though the messages traveled from the couple to their lawyer and then to us. Even so, I always felt a small sense of trepidation when I saw the lawyer's return address in my inbox—would this be the e-mail that brought bad news?

The fact that the woman was having weekly ultrasounds alarmed me—it's unusual to have so many. I learned that she'd experienced a mild complication, reminding me of the one I'd had in my pregnancy with the girls, and we were glad her obstetrician was being extremely vigilant. I renewed my prayers that she'd have a safe and healthy pregnancy.

We continued to ask Ellen if she could tell us anything to lift the veil of mystery shrouding the other couple. We were told that they were active and well-known in their community. Ellen added that they were "deeply religious."

I had suspected they might have a religious reverence for life when we learned that they planned to continue the pregnancy. Many people, even religious ones, would not have hesitated to assume that this pregnancy somehow fell outside God's will and would've arranged for an abortion. A woman can say she's pro-life, but when her emotions get all tangled up in her situation, especially if there's a risk to her health, it's easy to set aside personal convictions.

It's easy to talk the talk—but the woman carrying our child was walking the walk. And we would always be grateful to her.

If the situation were reversed, I could never have ended someone else's pregnancy. If I'd done so, I'd have struggled under a burden of guilt for the rest of my life.

After every e-mail, Ellen asked the other couple's lawyer when we might be able to meet them. I had told her I would be willing to wait until the second trimester, when the constant threat of miscarriage would have eased, but I wanted to at least know who these people were before the birth. They were taking care of our baby!

The days and weeks continued to drag. Then, on April 16, Paul and I received a surprise—the other couple's attorney reported that her clients would be willing to meet with us at her office on April 27. "Just name the time," we told her, "and we'll be there."

We'd have to drive to Toledo, but I knew the miles would fly by. We were so excited. Within a few weeks, we'd meet the other couple. We could establish a connection, meet them face-to-face, and hopefully exchange names and contact information. Finally we were making progress. I thanked God, reminded that he was working in ways we couldn't know.

Later that afternoon we received another e-mail with an ultrasound picture from the woman's appointment on April 14. The baby had reached the twelve-week milestone, marking the end of the first trimester.

I was sitting on our bed when I read the e-mail. Overcome with a sense of relief, I looked up and grinned at my husband. "Hey, Paul, I think we're going to have a baby."

We were now entering the safe zone, when the risk of miscarriage is not as high as it is during the first trimester. Of course anything could happen at any time, but we were riding a wave of optimism.

Paul was even more optimistic than I was. Now that we'd safely passed through the first trimester, he wanted to start telling people that we were expecting; I wanted to continue to keep our secret. I was trying to protect myself, I know—I couldn't forget the pain and disappointment that follow when something goes wrong in a pregnancy. Plus, because our situation was so strange, I was uncomfortable discussing it. I knew people would ask questions I couldn't answer, and those questions would frustrate me and add to my stress. What were people supposed to say when we told them our news? "Congratulations"? For what? We didn't get pregnant. We didn't have the baby. I know that's the wrong attitude—the important thing is the baby, not the pregnancy—but I couldn't help feeling cheated.

Bottom line, I didn't know how to handle a pregnant/not pregnant scenario. This one was beyond the ordinary, a situation my *What to Expect When You're Expecting* book had never addressed. My goal was to protect my child's privacy. The possibility of our names and faces splashed across newspapers and television was a huge concern for me.

I'd been through a pregnancy, and this wasn't at all the same thing. Neither was it like an adoption, because we were waiting for our biological child—the one that should be growing in my belly. The situation was, in a word, extraordinary.

∽

A few days later, Ellen and I spoke on the phone about our impending conference on April 27. She mentioned that the other couple's attorney had a formal agenda for the meeting.

Ellen asked me what we'd like to discuss.

"Well," I answered, "I really want to meet them and establish contact. I just want to know their names and open up the lines of communication."

We'd had several phone conferences since Paul and I had hired

Ellen, and she had proven to be an invaluable adviser. We were thrilled by the prospect of finally meeting the people who were caring for our baby.

On the twenty-seventh of April, Paul and I took time off from work and drove to downtown Toledo, eager and anxious. Finally we would be meeting the other couple. Finally we would be in the same town, the same building, and the same room as our baby.

We told our babysitter we had an out-of-town appointment, after which we planned on going out for dinner, so we thought we'd be home between seven and nine p.m. She gave me a confused look because we'd never asked her to come in at noon and work through dinner, but she didn't ask anything about where we were going. We didn't tell her either—we simply hugged the girls good-bye and left as soon as we could after the babysitter arrived. As we pulled out of town, Paul said he thought we were leaving the house too early, but I said it was better to arrive early than late.

A strange feeling settled over us as we drove south. We couldn't remember the last time we'd been alone together in the car, and it felt odd not to hear child noises from the backseat. I had printed directions in my lap and Paul had his GPS, but the two didn't agree with each other. Paul ended up going the way he thought best, and as a result we ended up in the midst of construction and had to take a confusing detour. Would we ever get there?

We parked several blocks away from the lawyer's office. After walking for about thirty minutes, we finally found the building and stepped into the elevator. As we rode up to the appropriate floor, I found myself wondering how we were supposed to introduce ourselves to the receptionist: *Hi, we're the genetic parents of the baby in one of your clients and we have an appointment to meet the gestational carrier?*

Maybe I'd just ask for their lawyer.

That's what we did. A little more searching revealed the right office, so we stepped inside and asked for the attorney by name.

I wasn't sure what to expect during this meeting, but I really wanted the other couple to see us as a normal, decent, hardworking couple. Paul would have been happy dressing in jeans and a polo shirt, but I told him he had to look nice, as if he were dressing for a business meeting. I recommended a sport coat, shirt, and tie. He thought I was nuts, but he agreed to wear khaki pants and a dress shirt.

I didn't know what to wear. I wanted to look slim and well put together, so I wore black from head to toe, thinking the color would make me look thinner. I felt as though I were about to meet my future in-laws or interview for an important job. I know this sounds crazy, but I was concerned that I wouldn't meet some unwritten standard and the other couple wouldn't approve of us. Maybe they'd decide to keep the baby!

More than anything, I wanted this couple to be glad they were doing this for us. I knew it would be hard to surrender a baby you'd carried and nurtured for nine months. I couldn't imagine the heartbreak of carrying a child, only to surrender it to a couple you didn't even like.

Our goal for that April meeting was simple: we wanted to meet the other couple, introduce ourselves, express our gratitude, and open the door to future communication. We hoped that we'd be able to speak directly with them without having to go through the lawyers. And of course we wanted to know their names.

We met our attorney in person for the first time that day. Ellen drove up from Cincinnati, and I met her in the restroom, of all places, where we shook hands when she introduced herself. I told her how excited Paul and I were to finally meet her and the other couple.

We met the couple's lawyer in a small conference room. She smiled, probably in an attempt to relax us, and said, "Carolyn's really nervous and hopes you'll talk first."

Carolyn—finally I had a name!

"No problem," I said, hoping I didn't look as nervous as I felt. "I can talk first."

Since we had been waiting two and a half months to meet these people, I had no problem speaking first. I had a lot to say.

The lawyer explained that they were still setting up the room— the thought of world leaders meeting in a formal United Nations assembly flashed through my brain—so we could chat for a few more minutes. She mentioned that she had a formal agenda and planned to follow it. The meeting would be very businesslike and shouldn't hold any surprises.

Paul and I assured her that we were fine with that approach. We were open to anything, and we'd tell the other couple anything they wanted to know. We simply wanted to be able to call them by name instead of thinking of them as "the other couple."

Finally we all drew deep breaths and approached the office where the lawyer's clients—and our unborn baby—waited.

When we stepped through the doorway, my eyes were automatically drawn to the other woman's face. A lovely woman, Carolyn was slender—so slender that if I hadn't known, I never would have guessed she was pregnant. She had shoulder-length blond hair and was classically dressed in a navy blue blouse, a matching skirt, and an elegant string of pearls. She looked exactly as I had pictured her. Her husband was dressed in a blue sport coat, light blue dress shirt, tie, and khaki pants. As a couple, he and Carolyn complemented each other.

The couple stood up when we entered and reached out to shake our hands. I took Carolyn's hand in mine, oddly aware that with this flesh-to-flesh touch I was finally linked to our baby. A couple of other people were also in the room—both were lawyers with the firm.

We went around the circle and made polite introductions. The couple across from us introduced themselves as Sean and Carolyn. Later on in the meeting, we finally learned their last name: Savage.

Paul and I said, "Good to finally meet you," and smiled. Though the atmosphere was tense and they seemed to smile reluctantly, I was relieved to meet them in person. I couldn't believe I would soon be spilling my heart and soul in front of these people.

We sat down, and everyone seemed to look at me. Supposing that was my cue to begin talking, I took a deep breath and began by telling the Savages thank you. "We are so thankful," I said, looking at Carolyn. "I hope you know that." I talked a little about how hard this had to be for her, but the woman across the table seemed somewhat removed. We made eye contact, but she looked stressed and her husband rarely smiled. I couldn't help feeling like I was doing my best to impress a personnel director and not getting a lot of feedback from the interviewer. The other couple simply looked at us as I rattled off all the things I wanted to say. At times I thought Carolyn was going to burst into tears or become ill. Sean sat and listened with a stoic look on his face. I kept thinking, *Oh, this isn't going well. They're not impressed.*

I talked for about ten minutes, and then Sean, the husband, spoke up. Paul was surprised that Sean spoke for the entire family.

"Usually I can't get a word in edgewise when Shannon is talking," Paul says. "But the atmosphere was chilly in the beginning, and if it hadn't been for Shannon opening up and pouring her heart out, the meeting may not have turned out so well."

Sean explained that they decided not to terminate the pregnancy right after they found out about the mistake. He asked a couple of questions about our experience with the fertility practice—obviously he and his wife were trying to figure out what had happened at the lab.

We shook our heads, sharing our mutual angst, and for the next ninety minutes we each told our stories. We shared how we learned the news, and related how we planned to tell people about what had happened.

Then Sean said something I will never forget: "Pregnancy is a public event." He went on to say that they couldn't hide Carolyn's condition, and they didn't want to live a lie. He mentioned that their family was well-known in Toledo, and between their involvement at work, church, and school, it would be impossible to hide from everyone. They wanted to tell the truth, so they had decided to have a family meeting and explain the situation to everyone at once.

With guidance from our lawyers, the four of us went over how our situation should progress. We would continue to exchange e-mails, but Ellen asked if we could communicate more directly. Perhaps we could establish e-mail accounts just for the purpose of exchanging messages with one another.

I was growing weary of interacting through lawyers, but the Savages weren't quite ready for direct e-mails or an exchange of phone numbers.

I smiled across the table. "Why don't we do this—we'll give you everything—e-mail addresses, home phone, work phones, cell phones, and complete address—and you can call us at any time. And if you're willing to give your contact information to us, we promise not to intrude on your lives."

The Savages' lawyer delicately changed the subject by asking if we should discuss where the baby should be born. If Carolyn gave birth in Ohio, could we drive down for the event? Of course we could.

The Savages expressed a desire to have amniocentesis with DNA testing to be absolutely sure the lab mistake wasn't part of an even larger error—what if some other couple was involved in this? A DNA test would also rule out the possibility that the baby wasn't theirs. I voiced concern about the amnio, not because I doubted what the doctors had told us, but because having an amnio is not without risk. Prior to the meeting, Ellen had told us that genetic proof would help us with the judge when the time came to issue the birth certificate in our names.

"I don't mind the DNA testing," I repeated, "but would rather have it done *after* the baby's birth."

Reluctantly I agreed that if an amnio would settle all questions of paternity before the baby's birth, then it should be done. Paul would have to get a DNA test. If the results of his test were compatible with the baby's, all lingering doubts would be erased.

Almost without warning, Carolyn began to talk. As if someone flipped a switch inside her, she pulled out several pages of notes and began to work through her list. She talked about her medical history and her difficulties with past pregnancies.

I sat back, suddenly realizing that I had fewer complications carrying the twins than Carolyn had in her last pregnancy. My sense of comfort vanished and my concern for Carolyn's health grew. As she talked, however, she began to relax. She told us about their children and their quest to expand their family.

Encouraged by her new openness, I mentioned that I'd like to get the lawyers out of the way and e-mail her directly.

She stiffened slightly. In a reserved tone, she said that she hadn't wanted this meeting. She would have been fine without ever meeting us.

I didn't know how to respond. Feeling embarrassed, I thanked her again and told her we merely wanted to express our gratitude.

One of the attorneys concluded the meeting. We said our farewells, walked out, and went to have dinner with Ellen.

At dinner, Ellen asked if we were happy with how the meeting went.

"Yes," I answered, "because our main objective was to meet the other couple and extend our gratitude. It would have been nice to begin establishing a relationship, but that's okay. They are at least sharing medical updates with us, and they are willing to work with us. I can't expect her to invite me to ultrasounds and become my best friend overnight. We'll take this one day at a time."

We didn't know if we'd see the Savages again until the birth. Though we'd given them all our contact information, we still didn't know if they'd be willing to reach out to us.

But this meeting was enough; it had to be. We had met the woman caring for our child, so Peanut was no longer floating aimlessly in our imaginations. He was inside Carolyn Savage, a generous woman who had committed to nurturing him for the duration of the pregnancy.

We should have been able to relax at that point, but the meeting had exhausted us. I'd been so nervous that I developed a tension headache that lasted three days.

But knowing Peanut was in safe hands was worth it all.

Chapter Ten

One Step Closer

April melted into May while Paul and I remained frozen in a state of cautious waiting. It wasn't a happy time, but at least it was a hopeful time. We felt as though we were living under a cloud of uncertainty, and we didn't want to share our news lest we spread that uncertainty and cause others to worry. The fewer people who knew, we reasoned, the better.

We chose to exercise great care when it came to our relationship with the Savages. Like most people, we didn't become instant friends overnight, and in the beginning we didn't want to push too hard. We planned to be as respectful of their privacy as they were of ours. We wanted to know about Carolyn's health, especially since she had three other children who depended on her. I suppose you could say we were trying to be as sensitive as possible.

Not only were we concerned about the Savages, but we also had to decide how to deal with the people who were closest to us. How much should we tell them? When should we tell them?

When the twins were born, we told only my parents and sister that they were conceived through in vitro. Our reticence to share the news didn't stem from embarrassment, humiliation, or self-pity. Our hesitation was based on the fact that we felt *exposed* by sharing such intimately personal details with other people. Some things ought to remain private, right? Plus I never wanted people to look at my children and single them out because of their unique conception. *Test-tube baby* is not a term I ever wanted applied to my kids.

Now we struggled with the issue of how to share the news of this miracle baby without revealing our private affairs. I didn't want everyone in the world—even close personal friends—to know such details of my personal medical history. I didn't want to lie about the situation, so I couldn't say we adopted. I suppose I could have said that we used a gestational carrier, but I knew that statement would only invite questions about what a gestational carrier is and why we decided to use one. One of the friends to whom I had confided our situation suggested that I simply tell people we'd had complications and had to use a surrogate. People might wonder about the complications, but most people are well mannered enough not to ask about such personal things.

One afternoon my friend Deanna and I had lunch in my room and we talked about how to explain my sudden baby. "You could wear one of those empathy bellies for a while," Deanna said, laughing. "They look real."

"Yeah, but what if one of my students saw it?" I answered. "Explaining a fake belly would be harder than explaining a sudden baby. Plus people always come up and rub your belly when you're pregnant, and would an empathy belly *feel* like a real belly? I don't think so."

"Where would you even get one? Can you order one online?"

I pulled my laptop over, laughing at the crazy idea. Sure enough, a minute later I had found a site to order them, official empathy bellies for one hundred and fifty dollars.

"People would think I was nuts," I told her, closing the computer lid. "There's no way I could seriously consider that."

I was still carrying a few pounds from my first pregnancy, so I considered avoiding people all summer, wearing loose-fitting tops in the fall, and then reacting as if the baby had arrived early . . . but what if this was a big, full-term baby?

Or I could simply say that we'd had a miracle baby and leave it at that. People could come up with their own explanations, though probably none of them would be correct.

I knew only one thing for sure: I never wanted to go public with the complete story of how our baby was conceived and carried. And I certainly didn't intend to say anything until he was safely in our arms. The only control I could exercise in this situation was choosing who to tell, and when to tell them.

After pondering these things for long periods, I'd rake my hands through my hair and sigh. I could do nothing until the baby arrived, so we'd have to see how the situation unfolded. At this point, all we could do was wait.

Despite the formal and businesslike tone of our first meeting, our relationship with the Savages began to warm up and become friendly. By early May, Carolyn had established a special e-mail account through which she and I could correspond. I was thrilled—finally we could connect directly.

The first e-mail she sent was somewhat formal, giving us instructions on where and how Paul should give his DNA sample. She also gave me her phone number and said I could give her a call if I wanted to talk.

Did I! The first time we talked on the phone, we spoke for at least ninety minutes about all kinds of things other than the baby. We discussed the fertility clinic, we spoke about our experiences with reproductive technology, and we puzzled over what could have possibly caused this mix-up. We didn't share much about our personal lives, but instead focused on technical things. I found it easier and more relaxing to talk to Carolyn when just the two of us were involved in the conversation.

Carolyn prepared to have amniocentesis, a procedure in which a long needle would be inserted into the amniotic sac, the place where the baby lives and grows. Because fetal cells move freely in this liquid environment, doctors can analyze the baby's genetic makeup from a sampling of those cells. I knew Carolyn might experience some cramping from the procedure, so I prayed she'd be okay and the baby wouldn't be harmed.

A few days after the amnio, Carolyn sent us an e-mail saying that the results had come in on a Friday afternoon, but that she and

Sean had been on a jet when the lab left a telephone message. "I'll call them first thing Monday morning," she promised.

That was one of the longest weekends of our lives. Paul and I went to work as usual on Monday, but I had a preparation period in the morning. I called Carolyn at nine, before she'd had a chance to call the lab, so she promised to do it right away. A few minutes later she called back with the news—our baby was fine, genetically perfect. And our baby was a boy!

Paul would have been happy with another girl, but when he heard we were having a boy, his first thought was: *Now our family is complete.*

"When I saw the first ultrasound of the girls," he once told me, "I thought they were boys, but later I learned that Baby B was a girl. I thought that'd be perfect—one boy and one girl—but then I learned Baby A was a girl too. Now I can't imagine life without my little girls, but you have to understand, Shannon—your family is female-dominated; when you get together it's like living in a sorority house. We have two girls and all the aunts and uncles have girls, except for one family that has a son. So I was happy to hear that Peanut was a boy. He'll bring some balance to the force."

I was happy to hear the results too, yet one unavoidable doubt remained in my mind—the genetic tests they performed couldn't tell us if Peanut had problems with his hearing. We'd have to wait until after his birth to learn if, like Ellie, he'd been born deaf.

⁋

I've always thought of DNA tests as being done in a medical, discreet, and professional environment, but Paul soon found himself involved in a DNA adventure. Providing a DNA sample is a simple matter; in most cases, it simply involves a quick cheek swab with a stick resembling a giant Q-tip.

Paul didn't think the procedure would be a big deal, but it did provide him with one of the most unexpected journeys he's ever taken. Paul found himself driving to an office in an industrial part of town. He thought he'd find it in a flash, but he drove past the address three or four times without seeing any building that looked appropriate.

Finally he got out his GPS and punched in the address, but it kept telling him, "You are there." He got out of his van, then walked down an alleyway until he saw a steel door at the back of a nondescript building. The heavy industrial door had a window in it, the kind they used in the old speakeasies where visitors had to give a password before they'd be admitted.

What in the world?

Paul knocked on the door, twice, but no one answered. Was the place even open? He reached for his phone, then stopped to double-check the address, the time, the date. Yes, he was in the right place on the right date and at the right time. So he waited another moment and then *pounded* on the door.

Finally a woman's voice came through the window. "Can I help you?"

Paul said, "Is this . . ." and then he mentioned the name of the lab.

"Yeah."

"Well, I have an appointment for eleven forty-five."

"Are you Paul?"

"Yes." The door opened, revealing an older woman in jeans and a work shirt.

"It's after twelve. You're late."

Paul laughed. "Well, you don't exactly advertise your location. It's hard to find this place."

"Hang on, just a minute. I was about to leave."

Paul stepped into a white-painted hallway that looked like it was coated with primer instead of paint. Some walls were covered, others weren't. A few pieces of furniture—some chairs, a desk—were scattered about. The rest of the room was unfinished and didn't look like it'd ever be finished. Despite the haphazard appearance, security cameras hung from every corner, which meant someone somewhere was watching . . . for what?

The woman who'd let him in leaned against the edge of the desk and looked Paul over. "Fill out this paperwork," she finally said, handing him an assortment of pages. "Do you have your case number?"

Carolyn had sent us the case number, so Paul sat in a chair and began to fill out paperwork that asked for his driver's license number and other identifying information. When he'd finished, the woman took the papers and Paul looked up, expecting to be led into another room or to meet a medical professional from some other part of the building.

"Okay, follow me," the woman said. They walked into a small room that had a countertop and sink. Old cabinets surrounded the sink, and a line of duct tape ran across the floor.

"Stand with your back to the wall, place your feet on the taped line, hold up your ID and case number. Don't smile, it confuses the software program."

Paul did as he was told, feeling like a criminal prepping for his mug shot, while the woman grabbed a camera and took a few pictures. He looked around, wondering where the guy in the white lab coat was, but then the woman took out a cotton-tipped swab that looked like something you'd find on special at Rite Aid.

"Open," she said, gesturing to Paul's mouth as she walked toward him.

He opened his mouth. She slid four of the swabs between his gums and his cheek, dropped them into a waxed paper bag, and put the bag in a large envelope. She asked Paul to sign a letter certifying that he hadn't put anything else in the envelope, and they were finished.

Paul stared at her, confused. "Is that it? Just swabs in a bag?"

She cackled a laugh. "You want more?"

Where am *I?* Paul wondered, but the woman dropped the letter and swabs into a FedEx envelope and that was the end of that.

∽

After the reports from the amnio came back, we had to wait another seven to ten days for the results of the DNA test. Carolyn would receive the results. We expected the report to reveal that Paul was the father, which meant that Carolyn and Sean could not be the biological parents.

The days dragged by and we didn't hear anything. Finally I followed up with an e-mail to Carolyn. "Have you heard anything? Shouldn't we have heard something by now?"

Carolyn e-mailed that there'd been some kind of holdup—apparently the lab didn't think they had received the payment for Paul's test. They had received the check, of course, but it had been misapplied, so after they straightened out the problem we finally got the lab results.

Carolyn phoned me one morning. She told me they had received the report on their genetic testing, but that she almost threw out the envelope, thinking it was junk mail. The tone of her voice shifted to a more serious note. She said the DNA results were conclusive: she and Sean had no genetic connection to the baby she was carrying.

Though I had anticipated this result, I was even more anxious to learn about Paul's test, the results of which would come to us in the mail. What if he wasn't the father? Then what? I thought the clinic was sure Carolyn was carrying was our child, but what if she wasn't?

It's a good thing I went through our mail carefully because Carolyn was right—the results arrived in a nondescript envelope I could have easily mistaken for junk mail. My hands shook as I opened the letter—were we the parents of this child or not? I skimmed the page in one quick glance, then grinned in a surge of relief. Paul Morell was a 99 percent match. No doubt about this boy's father!

I immediately called Paul, Carolyn, and Ellen, knowing they would all be relieved at this news. Another piece of the puzzle clicked into place.

I never asked Carolyn what she felt when she read the results of her DNA test, but I can imagine. Even as I prayed that the tests would go smoothly and confirm our parentage, had she been praying the opposite? I wouldn't have blamed her if she had been.

⁏

In early June I received another e-mail from Carolyn. She related that she and Sean had realized that they had not spoken to us about their intentions regarding ongoing contact with our child.

She gently made it clear that she and Sean didn't expect any further contact. An occasional general update and picture would be appreciated, but they did not plan on developing or encouraging a relationship with our son. Their job was to safely carry and deliver him. Our job was to be his parents.

I wrote her back right away:

Carolyn,

That sounds reasonable. I'd be happy to give you annual updates. I really hadn't thought about the next step yet. I didn't expect you to establish a relationship with the baby, though I'm not opposed to it either. When the time is right, years down the road, I imagine I'll have to explain to our son why he was born in Ohio and not Michigan. It's then when maybe he might want to meet you. Though, who knows, he may not want to. It's really hard to speculate on this.

. . . I did feel better once we met in person. I know you are taking care of yourself and getting the best medical care. You've also made it clear that we're the parents. It's all still odd, and nothing can change that fact. We remain appreciative and grateful that you didn't end the pregnancy.

This has been a difficult few months for everyone. I don't have any expectations of you or Sean after the baby's birth. Your role after the birth is totally up to you. So I'd be happy to send photos or an occasional e-mail. If you ever want to meet him in person, that's fine too. When he's old enough to understand this situation, I'll tell him.

Shannon

In a typical pregnancy, the mother-to-be suffers through a bit of morning sickness, but the nausea and discomfort are quickly forgotten in the thrill of the first quickening, the first kick. She shares these movements, this proof of life, with her husband and other children, if she has them, so the entire family can participate in the miracle of birth. The mother talks about baby names and shops for baby clothes, and she answers questions from the other children about what the baby will look like and what he might do after he arrives. Privately she dreams of how he will grow and what he might one day become. . . .

I missed out on nearly all those things. Until we knew about Peanut, I hadn't realized how important it is for prospective mothers to share their news with family and friends. Not only was my womb empty, but my heart felt empty too, as though I was missing out on an important part of my son's life.

When I first found out about the baby, I pulled out my pregnancy books and subscribed to an e-mail service that updates prospective mothers on their baby's week-by-week development. Now I had to put the books away and unsubscribe from those e-mails. All the printed materials detailed how and what I should be feeling, and I wasn't experiencing any of those sensations. I found it simply too painful to follow along. I closed the book, deleted the e-mails, and tried not to think about my son growing inside another woman.

At one time or another, most infertile women have to deal with the problem of baby showers. I discovered I could be supremely happy for the woman who's being honored, but beneath my happiness for her lay a bedrock of sorrow that couldn't always be disguised. At work, the teachers always give a baby shower for first babies, and I went to one during our time of waiting. A couple of people present knew about my situation, but they were keeping my secret. At that point we had safely passed through Peanut's first trimester, so I was cautiously optimistic.

Sitting in that circle of women, however, I began to wonder how I was going to tell people at work about my baby's birth. I would need time off for maternity leave, but that request would require personal details I really didn't want to give. I would have to come up with some kind of explanation, though, and soon.

We had to consider other issues as well. For two years I had been mentally preparing to give birth to another child or children, but Paul and I couldn't agree on names. We certainly couldn't call our son Peanut his entire life. We discussed possible names in hushed tones, secretly debating the identity of our undercover child.

Occasionally during this time Paul would come up behind me, rub my stomach, and tease me by saying, "How's our baby doing?"

I'd smack his hand away, because I couldn't see anything funny in the situation. I couldn't understand how my husband remained so happy and optimistic. I was living with an empty womb, though I thought about our baby every hour of every day. If only I could detach myself from the pregnancy, lock my maternal instinct in a closet, and throw away the key . . .

One afternoon my frustration grew to the point where I had an epiphany. I was driving home from school, my negative thoughts about the entire situation spiraling out of control, when I realized that I had to break free from obsessive angst. I gripped the steering wheel with both hands and gave myself a stern lecture: *You need to pull yourself together and deal with this. You can't think about what might have been. You've got to block those thoughts and deal with what is. So what is true and good?*

We were going to have a baby! A long-awaited answer to prayer. Certainly not the way we had anticipated, but the gift of our child was reason to celebrate. I could focus on my kids, my job, my home, and my husband. I could think about the future, not the past, and simply do my best to get through each day, focusing on what God was accomplishing—even though his ways mystified me.

I'd like to say I never fell back into my negative thoughts, but that wouldn't be true. That empty feeling occasionally slammed into me with the force of a fist, followed by worry, which nibbled at my resolve. Would the pregnancy be full-term? Would the baby be able to hear? Why would God do this? To save my life? To save Peanut's? There had to be a reason that this baby was coming into the world in such an unorthodox way. I didn't know what that reason was, but God did. For now, that would have to be enough.

Chapter Eleven

The Announcement

In late May, Paul and I decided the time had come to tell our immediate families about our unusual pregnancy. I told my sister first, on the phone. Though she was surprised and shocked, she reacted calmly.

In early June, my parents came to visit us. My mom and dad were both born in June, so we planned to celebrate both birthdays together. I thought that would be the perfect opportunity to tell them our news.

I had considered a million different ways to share the news; now I had only to open my mouth, gather my courage, and drop the bombshell. We were all sitting at our kitchen table when I decided the right moment had come. Dinner was finished, I was preparing to serve dessert, and the girls were playing in the living room. I glanced at Paul, then launched into our story. "We've got some news to tell you," I said. "We're going to have a baby. But . . . I'm not pregnant."

My mother shot me a puzzled look.

"Remember those six frozen embryos?"

She nodded.

"Well, in February we were told that they'd been thawed and three were transferred into another woman. One of those embryos implanted, so we're having a baby. It's a boy. He's due in October."

Paul and I watched as expressions of shock, disbelief, and joy flitted across my mother's face. She smiled and crossed her arms. "That's great. I'm sure thrilled at the thought of more grandchildren."

My dad sat quietly with a puzzled look on his face. I knew he had to be wondering how such a thing could happen.

Once the shock subsided, both parents had questions: "How did this happen? When did you find out? Why didn't you tell us sooner? How do you know the baby is really yours? Have you met the other couple? What's their name? Do they have other kids? Do they still have embryos? Does anyone else know about this? Do you have a lawyer? How did you choose the lawyer?"

We answered their questions as best we could, then warned them that they were to tell no one what had happened. My mom asked about our legal rights, and I explained that even though we'd hired a lawyer to represent us, we shouldn't have any problem asserting our rights since DNA proved we were the genetic parents. "It's actually good that the other family lives in Ohio," I explained, "since the laws there are more favorable toward surrogacy." We shared that we had met the other couple in April and they seemed like nice people who were committed to getting excellent medical care for the mother and the baby.

Mom said, "They sound like wonderful people. I'd love to meet them someday."

Paul wanted to tell more people, but I wanted to wait until after the baby was born. But since an instant baby would be truly shocking, I agreed that we should tell most people at least a month before the baby's birth.

Paul chose the following weekend to tell his mom about her coming grandchild. When he came home and mentioned that he'd shared our secret, I panicked at the thought of the story spreading. "Did you warn her not to tell anyone else? You need to call her right away and make sure she doesn't tell anyone else."

Sometimes I felt like we were on some kind of spy mission, all of us duty-bound to hide the Secret Baby.

"Telling my mom was interesting," Paul later told me. He didn't think the news would upset his mother—she used to be a nurse, so nothing fazes her.

"The three of us were sitting at the table after lunch," Paul recounted. "Me, my mom, and her husband, Charlie. Our conversation is usually mundane chitchat about how the tractor's running or about things on the farm. Mom was her usual super-calm self, so I was curious to see what her reaction to this news would be.

"We were sitting there digesting the meal, and I wondered if I should say anything, but knew this would be the ideal time to bring up the subject of the baby. So finally I said I had a bit of news.

"Mom's eyes met mine. 'Yes?'

" 'We're expecting a baby boy,' I told her.

" 'Oh . . . wow. You know it's a boy?'

" 'Yes.'

" 'When's it due?'

" 'September or October.' "

The words fell like stones into calm water, stirring only a few small ripples. Charlie sat chewing and Paul's mom nibbled on a cookie while he thought, *Okay, this is the turning point.*

"The thing is," he added, clearing his throat, "this isn't a normal pregnancy."

His mom choked on her cookie and tilted her head, interest flashing in her eyes. "Oh?"

"Yeah. First of all, we went through in vitro fertilization for the twins. Normally, Shannon would go in, they'd transfer the embryo, and the baby would grow inside her."

His mother waited, eyes expectant.

"But a mix-up happened at the lab and Shannon's not carrying our child."

The three of them sat and stared at one another, then Paul's mom said one word: "Really?"

"Yeah, really. A woman in Ohio is carrying our child for us, and we're not sure when she's going to go into labor." Paul gave them a few more details, and ended with a warning. "We're trying to keep it quiet because there are some legal issues involved, so don't tell anyone."

His mother smiled. "As long as everything's okay."

"I knew Mom was the hub," Paul told me. "With five brothers and sisters, she's the one who communicates with all the family members. She's raised six kids in a big traditional Catholic family, and she's been through all kinds of crazy stuff. I knew she could handle this. She can ride the waves of almost any storm.

"And she was really happy to hear we were having a boy. Only one other person in our entire family tree has a boy to carry on the name."

Paul's mom did tell one of his brothers, but he kept the news secret. Paul's brother called once to see how we were doing, but we didn't have much news to tell him. We were still waiting and praying, all we could do.

Before school dismissed for the year, I went to my principal's office and closed the door behind me. In as few words as possible, I told her what had happened and asked her not to tell anyone.

My desire for privacy stemmed from our wish to protect our child. Someday Paul and I would sit down with him and tell him his story, but we wanted to be the ones to do that.

Maybe we were being naive, but we were sure of one thing: we didn't want him to discover the circumstances of his birth on the Internet.

Chapter Twelve

Preparing for Peanut

By the time we flipped the calendar to July, everything in our lives seemed to be progressing well. School had dismissed for summer break, and I planned to take advantage of this time off to do some serious preparation for the baby. Carolyn wasn't due until October, but she'd had other babies early—one at thirty weeks and another at thirty-two.

I experienced a few embarrassing moments while shopping for baby clothes. I'd have several items in my arms—obviously more than I'd buy for a shower gift—and someone would come up and start talking about babies. Or they'd ask, "When's your baby due?" Some even looked at my belly and added, "You look really good for being that far along."

I learned to say, "Thanks" and move on. I didn't want to explain everything to everyone I met.

In midsummer I visited my dermatologist. I've been his patient since I was fifteen, so he's known me a long time.

"I don't understand why I'm having so many problems with my

skin," I told him as I settled into his chair. "I'm having all kinds of breakouts."

He peered at me and agreed that my skin didn't look good. He flipped through my chart. "I haven't seen you in two years. What's going on with you?"

I hesitated. "Nothing . . . much."

"Are you under more stress than usual?"

I opened my mouth to assure him everything was fine, and then the truth came tumbling out. "Actually, I have been under a lot of stress. Remember me telling you about my twins?"

He nodded. "I do."

"Well, I also had frozen embryos. But in February, the clinic told me that my embryos had been thawed. They were transferred into another woman and she's currently pregnant with my child."

He blinked, and then shook his head. "Well, that explains a lot. Acne can erupt months after an initial period of stress."

Apparently my case proved his point.

Back at the house, Paul and I prepared the baby's room. We'd had the girls in separate bedrooms, but we moved Megan into Ellie's room and repainted the walls because I wanted to make it special for their new room. I gave Megan a paintbrush and let her help me cover the walls in cotton candy pink so she could participate in the process of preparing for her new room with Ellie. The baby's room became a beautiful sky blue.

The girls still didn't know they had a baby brother on the way. We wanted to transition them into their new sleeping arrangement well before the baby arrived. I didn't want Megan to think her baby brother had pushed her out of her room.

One of our neighbors was pregnant with a baby boy, so we made a big deal about him with the girls. Much to my surprise, Megan kept asking when she was going to have a baby brother . . . and she was more right than she realized. That summer, not a day went by that she didn't ask, "Mommy, when am I going to have a baby brother?" I didn't give her a definite answer, though, or she would have told the world.

Chapter Thirteen

How Could I Say No?

Toward the end of July, Carolyn asked if I wanted to come down for her next ultrasound. The unexpected invitation excited me. The timing wasn't ideal, but how could I say no? I had been the one who wanted to establish a connection, and if I didn't go, she might not invite me again. I really wanted to be there, even though I was uncomfortable with the idea of intruding into a very personal time for Carolyn. So I e-mailed her back: *I'd love to go! What's the address?*

In early August, while Paul went to work, I left my girls with my parents and drove down to the city where the Savages lived. We had seen the baby on video—as Carolyn had prepared for a previous ultrasound, I'd asked if they could record it, and she had sent the DVD to me. That DVD held the first "live action shot" we had of our son.

Carolyn told me to meet her at the doctor's office at one, and I pulled into the parking lot at about twelve forty-five. I got out and went into the building, then waited for a while in the lobby. When she didn't show up, I told myself not to panic—had she told me to meet her in the lobby or in the reception area? I couldn't remember.

As the hands on my watch swung toward the hour, I decided to wait inside the doctor's office, so I went into the reception area and took a seat. The receptionist leaned over her desk and looked at me. "May I help you?"

"Oh, no." My cheeks grew warm. "I'm waiting for a friend."

I looked away, feeling ridiculous and totally out of place in the empty reception area. Where was Carolyn? Had I written down the wrong date? Was this the right office?

That's when it hit me—how many adult women ask a friend to accompany them for a medical checkup? None that I knew. For a moment I considered walking up to the desk and asking if Carolyn Savage had an appointment, and then explaining that I was the biological mother of Carolyn's baby . . . but no, I couldn't do that.

I walked down the hallway and peered over a balcony at the foyer below. Maybe I could go down and catch Carolyn at the door. But I didn't want to look like I was afraid she wouldn't come. So I paced the hallway for a few more minutes, then went back to the waiting room and flipped through a few magazines. I checked my watch, and then closed my eyes. I had to get out of there.

I decided to call Carolyn, but I had left her phone number in my van. As I walked toward the van to get my cell phone, I saw her drive up.

"I'm so sorry," she said when I approached. "I had the time wrong. The appointment isn't until one thirty."

At that point, I didn't care; I was just glad to see her. She looked great, and this time anyone could tell she was pregnant. I tried not to stare at her belly, though my eyes were magnetically drawn to the place where my baby was growing.

Because she'd arrived early, we sat together in the lobby for a while and made small talk about our families and how she was feeling. Her daughter, an adorable toddler, was with her.

Finally we went to the reception area. As Carolyn signed in at the desk, I wondered how much the staff knew about our situation.

Almost immediately a nurse led us into the ultrasound room. When Carolyn climbed up on the table and lifted her shirt, I was again struck by how personal this appointment was—maybe I should leave and give her privacy. When Sean walked in, I *really* felt like a third wheel. I didn't think the moment could possibly become more uncomfortable, but it did. Pregnancy wasn't supposed to be shared like this.

The technician pulled the curtain around us, but the setup wasn't very private. I was grateful Carolyn's daughter had come along— she distracted us and enabled us to talk about something other than the unusual situation that had bound us together.

The ultrasound technician began to point out the baby's body parts, so I leaned forward to watch the monitor and tried not to look at the couple behind me. "There's your baby's head," the technician said, nodding at the screen. "And there's his nose, do you see it?"

I drank in the image even as something within me wished she'd hurry so we could finish with this ordeal. If I had been the woman on the table, I would have made enthusiastic comments, but all I could do in this situation was murmur in agreement: "Yes, I see. Arm. Foot. Head."

If this was uncomfortable for me, how must Carolyn and Sean feel? Carolyn was the one with the transducer gliding over her belly, yet the technician was talking to me. I kept thinking that I shouldn't be there and wondered if I could make a quick getaway.

Thankfully the ultrasound was finished within a few minutes, but then we had to go to an exam room and wait for the doctor. As we left, the technician gave me, rather than Carolyn, pictures of the baby.

We waited for at least half an hour before the doctor arrived, passing the time by talking about how Carolyn was feeling and how we would handle things on the day of the birth. The atmosphere was uncomfortable . . . for me, at least. Because Carolyn, Sean, their daughter, and I were crowded into the small room, the walls seemed to close in on us as the moments dragged by.

The doctor finally came in. Carolyn introduced me, and the doctor said, "Nice to meet you." Then she turned her attention to her patient, and I listened to Carolyn tell her how she was feeling. Though the doctor talked to all of us, I kept wishing I could close my eyes and vanish. Carolyn and I had exchanged many e-mails, but we really didn't know each other well enough to share this kind of intimate experience.

Though Carolyn was carrying my baby, this was her appointment and her pregnancy. Everyone was friendly and kind, but still

I felt out of place. I'm a private person, not the sort to want family and friends in my delivery room, not the sort to want even close family members standing in at my doctors' appointments.

I thanked the doctor's staff as well as the Savages and told Carolyn we'd talk soon.

By the time the appointment was finished, I desperately needed to unwind. I went for something to eat, then walked into a department store and wandered aimlessly through the aisles, trying not to dwell on the fact that I had just viewed pictures of my baby in another woman's womb.

⁏

As the days of summer slipped by, Paul and I completed most of our preparations without explaining why they were necessary. A few weeks before our son was born, I began to talk to the girls about the baby. Paul had decided on a name, so the girls learned not about Peanut, but about their soon-coming baby brother, Logan.

"I went on a Web site of baby names and started scrolling through the list," Paul told me. "Normally, I hear a name and it will pop out, so this was a good way to have all the names thrown at me. I went through the lists alphabetically and didn't react to anything until I got to the L's. I didn't think I'd find anything there, but when I read Logan, the name just jumped out at me. It's a cool name."

When I heard Paul's suggestion for a name, I liked it, but told him teasingly that if he got to choose the first name, I wanted to choose the middle name. A few weeks later, I convinced him that

Logan's middle name should be Savage. Not only was it my maiden name and would honor my parents, but it would also honor Sean and Carolyn.

Watching the girls' excited anticipation as we talked to them about Logan, I finally began to allow myself to feel undeniable excitement. "I can help change diapers," Megan would say, and Ellie would add, "And I can give him a bottle."

The girls had very little sense of time, so I knew they wouldn't mind waiting awhile before Logan came home. I explained that one day we would go to the hospital and pick him up, and then he would come live with us.

In a way, the girls were a godsend. Between my job and taking care of them, I stayed busy. My mind and hands were almost always occupied. I began to make a point of doing special things with the twins so they'd have plenty of attention before the baby arrived. I signed them up for everything Gymboree had to offer: art, music, and play classes. We made weekly trips to Ann Arbor for Ellie's speech and audiology appointments. We went shopping and had lots of playdates. Once fall came, the girls would begin preschool, so I set out to make the most of every possible moment.

I didn't want to be guilty of wishing so hard for the future that I'd let the precious present slip through my fingers.

Chapter Fourteen

On His Way

In September, our situation began to get dicey. We learned that Carolyn had begun to have new complications. I grew tense with concern about her and the baby. Though she was carrying our child, she also had to care for her own three children. What if something happened to her? Paul and I spoke at length about this and were deeply concerned.

Carolyn thought the baby might come over Labor Day weekend, her thirty-second week. We went on alert over the holiday, but nothing happened. At this point, her doctor and a specialist were monitoring her twice a week, so we were on edge and apprehensive. Each day I woke up and wondered, *Is this the day our son will be born?* A delivery at thirty-two weeks meant he'd be rushed to the neonatal intensive care unit, or NICU. What physical challenges would he face?

At one point I asked Carolyn, "Is it harder for you to carry this baby than if it had been one of your own?"

"Yes," she answered, after a thoughtful pause. She told me that in a way, it felt like she was babysitting someone else's child. If your toddler drops her pacifier on the floor, you pick it up and stick it back in her mouth, but if someone else's child drops his pacifier, you wash it off before giving it back. That's the sort of responsibility she felt.

I understood what she meant. We're more relaxed with our own children than with someone else's because we're keenly aware of the responsibility that has been entrusted to us.

Carolyn told me she had a C-section scheduled for October 19, at thirty-nine weeks. She thought she would make it only to October 7, and she was being carefully monitored. If anything happened to put her or the baby at risk, her doctor planned to deliver right away.

Hearing about Carolyn's complications only made me more appreciative of her decision and more eager to pray for her. She was an accidental surrogate, and she'd never asked for this responsibility. Both of us had been violated physically and emotionally. We were dealing with different aspects of the same problem, but the situation wasn't easy for either of us.

❧

As summer officially drew to a close, Paul and I decided to tell our extended families at our annual Labor Day picnic. By that time we were carrying our cell phones nonstop and anticipating a phone call from Carolyn at any time.

Pulling relatives aside one by one, I told my cousins and uncle that Paul and I were having a baby. They greeted this news with the usual shock, confusion, and excitement. My cousin's wife was pregnant and due in March, so we celebrated her news too. By this time I felt more comfortable sharing the news within our family circle.

Some people in my family had never thought about in vitro fertilization, nor did they know we'd used in vitro to conceive Megan and Ellie. So I had to start from the beginning and explain the procedure so they could understand how the mistake had taken place. Judging from the looks on some of their faces, the world of reproductive technology was as alien as rocket science. They had simply never considered it.

That same weekend we attended another picnic for Paul's side of the family. I knew Paul had already told his mother, but I didn't know if she'd shared the news with his other brothers and sisters. As we were getting ready to leave, I asked Paul's sister: "Did you know we're going to have a baby?"

She smiled in surprise. "No, I didn't. When?"

"Any day now. The baby isn't due until next month, but we think he's going to arrive early."

When her brow crinkled in confusion, we sat down and I told her the entire story.

She was stunned. She hadn't known that our twins were conceived through in vitro. Because Paul's dad had twin brothers, people had simply assumed that twins ran in the family. Until that moment I would've been happy to let them make that assumption—

after all, it *could* have happened that way. Though the in vitro information surprised her, the embryo mix-up nearly left her speechless.

Seeing the surprise on Paul's sister's face reminded me that a lot of people find the idea of in vitro fertilization confusing. We'd lived with the reality for several years, but other people needed time to process the facts.

I wanted to give them time to absorb the full truth, but the clock was ticking. Our son was on his way.

Chapter Fifteen

A Public Event

I'll never forget Sean saying that pregnancy was a public event. Carolyn *had* to share the news, because everyone in her circle could see her pregnant belly. I, on the other hand, had nothing to show anyone, unless they wanted to examine the stress-induced lines on my forehead.

Adoptive parents may understand this feeling, but I don't think the average mother-to-be would realize how odd this feels. Adoptive parents invent their own preparation rituals: they shop for toys and clothes for the child, they share their good news with family and friends, and they gather together to celebrate the new family member's arrival. No one thinks them odd, and while they may encounter the occasional rude comment, their announcement doesn't usually result in people looking dumbfounded.

No one calls the newspaper to alert the media of the news.

On September 15 I received an e-mail from Carolyn. She asked me to call her, because there had been "some developments" in our situation, and she wanted to make us aware of them.

The hard fist of fear slammed into my stomach. What had happened? Was the baby in danger? Was Carolyn?

I tried not to imagine the worst as I dialed her number, but my mind was spinning with awful possibilities. Above my racing heart, a tiny voice in the back of my head whispered that I'd been right to brace myself for the worst possible scenario, that this couldn't possibly end well.

"Carolyn? This is Shannon. You asked me to call."

I listened, the phone clenched against my ear, as Carolyn explained that somehow the national media had gotten wind of our story. Someone had leaked it to the press. She said the local media in Toledo had been asking questions for two months, but she and Sean hadn't made any public comments.

"Two months? Why didn't you say something earlier?"

She replied that they hadn't wanted to worry us. But now all kinds of news organizations wanted to interview them, so they'd hired a New York public relations firm to help them deal with all the attention.

A *public relations* firm? I was so stunned I couldn't speak.

Carolyn told me they didn't want a lot of media attention but thought if they could get out ahead of the story, they could tell what had happened and maintain control over the content. They didn't want to be chased down the street by reporters.

I was flabbergasted by the Savages' decision and wished they had shared what they were thinking earlier. Paul and I would have had more time to prepare.

Though I tried to remain calm, my hands trembled as I listened and responded. How could this be happening? I thought maybe *someday* we'd tell our story to the world, but *now*, just weeks before the baby was supposed to be born? This couldn't be happening, not to us, not to our baby.

"Who?" I asked. "Who wants to talk to you?"

"The *Today* show." Carolyn told me not to worry, because I wouldn't have to talk. She and Sean would keep our identity private.

I swallowed hard. "When—when will this air?"

She replied that the show would air on Monday or Tuesday. A crew was coming Thursday to tape an interview.

I gasped. "Can't they wait until after the baby is born? Why do it now? What's your objective in going public? Why would you do it?"

She replied that she and Sean wanted to make sure this kind of mistake never happened to anyone else.

I asked if the *Today* show producer wanted to talk to us, and she said no, not now, and assured me she'd never give out our phone number. She kept emphasizing that she wouldn't mention our names, but I feared we could hide only so long once the story got out.

Somehow I managed to say good-bye, then I hung up the phone and burst into tears. When I regained a measure of composure, I called Paul at work. "Paul, our story has gone public. I just spoke with Carolyn and she said they were scheduling an interview with the *Today* show."

"What?" Disbelief echoed in his voice. "I thought they wanted privacy. At our initial meeting they stressed keeping everything private, but now they're going on national TV?"

"I know, it doesn't make sense to me either. Carolyn said that local reporters had been contacting them for the past two months, and now they're getting inquiries from national media."

"Did the *Today* show contact us?"

"No. Carolyn said she wouldn't divulge our names. But you know they'll want to hear the rest of the story, so eventually they'll want to talk to us. This is horrible! What do you think we should do?"

Paul sighed. "I'm wrapping things up here. Let's talk when I get home."

Later Paul told me that when he put the phone down, he couldn't help feeling that a massive tidal wave was heading right toward us. But what could we do? As soon as the Savages gave their interview, people would naturally wonder about the other couple. I was shocked that the private, reserved people we'd met back in April would even *think* about sharing their experience on national television.

My next call was to Ellen. I trembled as I dialed her number and ended up leaving a tearful message explaining that our story had reached the national media. What were we going to do?

I hung up and stared at the floor as a dozen different emotions tore at my heart. Paul and I had learned to care deeply for Carolyn and Sean, and we would feel eternally indebted to them, but we couldn't understand why they had agreed to speak to the press now. Why couldn't they have waited?

When Ellen returned my call, I told her what had happened and asked her what we should do. She wanted to know the source of the leak, but we couldn't give her an answer.

I had kept everything so private, I'd taken such pains to make sure our baby wouldn't be known as the "embryo mix-up baby," but now we were going to be exposed.

I didn't want to share my reproductive health with the world. I didn't want to expose my children to the press. We could keep our identity private for a while, but for how long? Though Carolyn had said she wouldn't reveal our names, I knew it was only a matter of time before the world found us.

Paul and I had talked at length about how we wanted to tell our son the story of his birth, and we knew we didn't want him to learn it through Google or some outdated news report. But once we knew the Savages were going to appear on national television, we had to wrestle with the question of whether we should remain quiet or go public. If we went public, we knew there'd be no going back to a life of anonymity.

Paul pointed out the risks in keeping silent. "The media could make up their own story about us and go with that," he said. "What if they get it all wrong?"

"We don't have to go public *now*," I pointed out. "But if we wait, how long could we hide?"

On September 17, which happened to be Paul's thirty-ninth

birthday, we celebrated quietly at home. I couldn't help thinking about Carolyn and Sean, who were supposed to be taping their interview for the *Today* show. What did they say? How would they be perceived?

Carolyn also had a doctor's appointment that day, so I was anxious to know the results of her exam. I knew our baby's birth was imminent. That night I checked my e-mail several times, hoping for an update, but I received no news from Carolyn.

As I walked into school the next day, Deanna waved at me. "How's it going?"

"You're not going to believe this," I told her, my voice flat. "The other couple is going public with the story."

"What?" Her face clouded with concern. "I'm so sorry, Shannon. Do you mean *public* as in—"

"They're going on the *Today* show."

"Oh." Her eyes widened. "What are you going to do?"

I shook my head. "They promised not to reveal who we are, so what can we do? Nothing."

That same day, the day after the taping, Carolyn called me and said the *Today* show did want to talk to us. She didn't give them our number, but instead gave me the name and contact information for the producer. If we changed our minds and were willing to tell our side of the story, all we had to do was call.

That weekend I told my family about the latest development with the media. They pleaded with me to stay quiet and not go public. "You'll never get them off your back," my mother warned.

My father urged me to consider my children's safety. Did I want reporters and photographers trying to snap pictures of our home? Of my kids?

Paul and I agreed with my parents—though our son had already been exposed, we didn't want to subject our girls to a horde of media people.

My sister thought I was silly for even considering going public. She pointed out that the world was filled with crazy people, and did I want them knowing where I lived? I agreed with her and promised that if we did tell our side of the story, we'd be careful to protect our children.

Paul and I spent every free minute debating the question—should we talk or stay quiet? What would be the consequences of both options? If we kept quiet, would we be able to keep our secret? If we spoke out, would the media eventually leave us alone?

After six long days of trying to figure out what would be best to do, we decided to do nothing. Soon everything would die down and we could get back to normal life. I certainly didn't want reporters coming to my school or showing up on our doorstep. After all, it wasn't like we were at war with the Savages—we were getting along fine and there was no controversy in our situation, so maybe the story would simply fade away like yesterday's news.

We prayed for guidance.

Chapter Sixteen

Sharing the News

On September 21, the day the *Today* show was scheduled to feature the interview with Carolyn and Sean, I stayed home from work because Ellie had a doctor's appointment in the afternoon. I also knew my nerves would be stretched as tight as a drum as I waited to watch the interview. I didn't know how I'd react—would the segment upset me? Would people at work be talking about what they'd seen on morning TV? I kept a wary eye on the television, and I kept thinking that this would be the day our lives changed forever.

One of most significant people I had yet to tell was our babysitter—she had no idea we were expecting a newborn. I didn't want to tell her too soon in case something went wrong. I was going to tell her the first week she came back to work in late August, but at that time she looked exhausted and I didn't want to add to whatever burdens she was carrying.

But a couple of days before the *Today* show aired I called our babysitter and finally told her the news. She greeted my announcement with complete silence, so I prodded her: "Are you shocked?"

"Yes," she answered, obviously flustered. "A baby!"

"He's due in a few weeks, but don't tell anybody, okay?"

She promised to keep our secret . . . but that secret was about to be broadcast across the nation.

An hour before the program I was so jumpy I was glad I wasn't standing in front of my students.

When the *Today* show began to present our story I settled onto the couch. Paul was at work, so he'd have to watch the video later. I was anxious the entire time; would they slip and say our names? Could someone have discovered that we were the genetic parents? The segment opened with a prerecorded piece on the Savage family, explaining the egregious error at the lab and revealing how the couple learned the news. The doctor had called Sean at his office, Sean related, and he worried about how he was going to tell Carolyn.

He went home to tell her in person. He found her in the bedroom and spilled the bad news in a rush of words. Carolyn yelled at him, "No, no! You're joking!" But after seeing that he was as pale as a ghost, she knew he was telling the truth. He wouldn't lie about a thing like that.

When asked what had been the hardest part of the ordeal, Carolyn looked at Sean and smiled. "I don't think we've hit the hardest part yet."

I knew what she meant. The hardest part would be the delivery, and then handing over the baby she'd nurtured for so many months.

The broadcast then switched to a live interview, with Meredith Vieira asking questions of Sean and Carolyn. Carolyn explained that the pregnancy had been hard, but that they'd been rooting for the baby the entire time.

"It's been difficult," Sean summarized, "but we feel we've made the right decision."

Carolyn told the national audience that they'd worked with a mental health professional who was helping them look at the situation as a gift for a family "we didn't know eight months ago."

"We have high hopes for him," she added, speaking of the baby, "but they're his parents, and we'll defer to their judgment on when or if they tell him what happened and any contact that's afforded us."

Before the segment ended, Carolyn added that they had found a gestational carrier to carry her frozen embryos and were in the process of finalizing those details.

Suddenly the interview was over. The program went to commercial, and I thought the interview went well. But as I watched I kept thinking that the opposite half of the story wasn't being told. Our experience differed completely, and people needed to know about the heartache of biological parents who lose their embryos and are forced to experience a vicarious pregnancy.

I leaned back on the sofa as exhaustion swept over me. I was tired of hiding this pregnancy. Plus Paul and I both figured it was only a matter of time before we were outed as the parents of the "mistaken embryo" baby. If we didn't go public, we'd forever wonder if someone was about to track us down and expose us without our consent. Did we want that fear hanging over our heads for years?

I picked up the phone and called Paul at work. "Did you see it?"

"No, not yet. How did it go?"

"I thought it went okay. Though at the end, I thought that people were probably wondering about the biological parents." I asked the question I'd asked a dozen times before: "What do you think, should we keep quiet or tell our side of the story?"

Paul and I again discussed our options. Paul thought we had no choice but to speak out. But I had so zealously guarded our privacy, it would be hard to let go of the secrecy I had worked to maintain.

No one asked us if we wanted to go down this path. We had talked about the remote possibility of telling our story, but we thought we'd do that months or even years down the road, after we'd had time to adjust to a new baby and recover from our emotional distress.

But like it or not, we knew the press would soon be heading in our direction. So Paul and I made the momentous decision to go public with our side of the situation. We wanted to make sure both sides of the story were presented correctly, and we wanted to make it clear that we would be eternally thankful to the Savages for their precious gift. We wanted to say that both families had been presented with extraordinary circumstances, but together we'd tried to do what was best for *our* baby.

We concluded that we couldn't hide our third child forever, and it was time to share our news with friends, family, and the world.

I thought, perhaps naively, that once we shared our story, media interest would die down and fade away. After all, conflict creates drama, and our story was more about cooperation than about conflict.

And maybe afterward, I reasoned, other fertility clinics would be forced to be a little more careful about how they handled those precious embryos. Maybe they'd think twice about the ramifications of their mistakes. And maybe couples who'd investigated in vitro would remember their frozen babies and thaw them for a pregnancy or donate them to another infertile couple.

God had blessed us; we'd soon have a son. If people could see two couples who put the health and well-being of a child before their own needs, maybe the story would restore a little civility to the news.

I reached up and pulled down the notebook where I'd written the number for the *Today* show. I made a quick call to Paul to confirm that this was what he really wanted to do. "Go ahead," he said. "Make the call."

So I picked up the phone. Trembling with nervous energy, I dialed the number and got the producer's voice mail. I left a message: "Hi . . . Carolyn Savage gave me your number. My name is Shannon Morell. I'm the biological mom of the child Carolyn is carrying. She said you'd like to speak with us. If you're still interested, we'd be happy to talk with you." I left our phone number and hung up.

I talked to Carolyn that afternoon and learned that she was feeling *very* pregnant. "I could have this baby as soon as Thursday or Friday," she warned. She'd had three other babies, so she had an instinct for how things were moving along.

I promised we'd be ready.

That evening the *Today* show producer returned my call. She thanked me for speaking with her, then began to ask questions. Yes, they wanted to do a segment with us. When could we do it? "The sooner, the better," I said, thinking of Carolyn and the baby. She was due to give birth any day and I wanted to tell our story and be done. Later we would decide to do it on Wednesday.

Things were so out of kilter that entire day—Paul and I were stressed over the national coverage of our situation, the girls were off their regular schedule, and we were concerned about Carolyn and the baby. Ellie and Megan sensed that something was up, and they were wired. We were all distracted from our usual routine.

By eleven thirty p.m., we were just getting the girls to bed when the phone rang. Carolyn was calling, and the sound of her voice sent alarm bells ringing in my brain. With panic in her voice, she said that her water had broken and she was on her way to the hospital.

My pulse quickened. "Okay. Don't wait for us. We'll be there as soon as we can."

I hung up the phone and waved frantically at Paul. "Oh my gosh, we're having a baby. Carolyn's water broke and she's going to the hospital. Quick, get a bag packed."

I was drowning in a tsunami of panic—the same feeling I'd felt the day my girls were born. I needed to do a thousand things, and

I needed to do them *now*. I tried to call my friend, a fellow teacher, so she could arrange a sub for me the next day. Then I called my babysitter and asked her to come over right away, then I dialed my parents and told them they needed to come relieve our babysitter and pick up the girls. We'd probably be in Toledo for the next couple of days, so they could take the girls to their house. My pulse was pounding, and the sound of tension and panic in my voice set off the girls. They did not want to go to bed; they wanted to go with Paul and me.

"You can't go with us," I tried to explain. "We're going to the hospital to get the baby."

"I want to see my baby brother," Megan cried, clinging to my leg. Ellie grabbed the other leg and joined in the chorus. "I want to go with you too."

I didn't think our babysitter would *ever* arrive. We had asked the poor woman to get out of bed, but she arrived at the house as we were throwing things together for the trip. Nine months of stress had come to a boil and the lid was about to blow off the pot.

Paul and I tossed some clothes in an overnight bag. I grabbed a few outfits for the baby, the camera, camcorder, and the laptop. Paul hauled the car seat from the garage, intending to install it later. As soon as the babysitter took charge of the girls, we jumped in the van and headed toward the interstate and Ohio.

We were a quarter of the way there when Sean called again. "It was a false alarm," he said, his voice heavy with relief. "Her water didn't break after all." With a chuckle he added, "We just wanted to see how fast everyone could get to the hospital. The doctor made it in twelve minutes."

I laughed, thanked Sean for the call, and motioned to Paul, signaling that he could turn the car around. Then I called my parents and told them to relax and go home. Finally we called our babysitter at the house and told her we'd be back soon.

ↀ

In order to lessen public scrutiny as much as possible, on Tuesday the twenty-second I went online and deleted my Facebook account. I also considered my coworkers—how should I break the news to them? I asked my principal, who thought it best that I make a brief announcement to the school staff so they'd be forewarned about what might happen in the near future. Otherwise, when they woke up Wednesday morning and heard the news, they'd be in for a surprise.

That announcement was difficult. I walked into a special after-school staff meeting and spoke to about fifty of my coworkers. "Some things have happened to me and my husband, and the news should hit the national media soon," I told them. "We're fine, but you should know a couple of things." I explained that my girls had been born through in vitro, we'd had frozen embryos mistakenly transferred into another woman, and our son was about to be born. "We're only doing a couple of interviews," I finished, "so we'd appreciate it if you didn't talk to anyone or comment if you hear the students talking about the situation."

As I explained, I was overcome by the horrible feeling that I'd stepped into a crowded waiting room and was publicly announcing the results of my gynecological exam.

After school, I went to a local park where Paul, the girls, and I taped a segment of "B roll" for the *Today* show producer to use in our interview. After the crew filmed us playing with the girls, Amy Robach, one of the show's correspondents, asked us a few questions for the preinterview. Our segment was scheduled to air on Wednesday the twenty-third.

I didn't sleep more than an hour that night because I was so worried about the live interview to come. I worried about oversleeping. I worried about looking exhausted on camera because we had to get up at four a.m. and drive to a nearby hotel for the interview. I had never been on local TV, much less a national broadcast. What if we messed up or said something silly? Should we rehearse?

I composed several likely questions and thought about my answers. I told Paul we should talk about questions they might ask. Paul gave me a *You've got to be kidding* look. "Shannon, I know the story; we've been living it for the past eight months. Why do I need to go over it?"

We discussed whether we should include our kids in the taping. I wanted to protect their privacy. If it had been left up to me, I wouldn't have included any photos or allowed the girls to be taped. Paul thought we should involve them; after all, the Savages' segment had included their children. Yet I didn't want to expose the girls. I worried about their safety.

The next morning we got up early and prepared for live television. The producer wanted us to arrive at the hotel by six fifteen, so we got ready in the dark. As I dressed, my mind raced as I imagined questions they might ask. Fortunately, my parents had picked up the girls the day before, so they were in good hands and safely away from the hubbub.

When Paul and I arrived at the hotel, the crew had set up in a large hallway. A continental breakfast buffet had been spread on a table, but I was so nervous I couldn't eat. I could have used some coffee, but I didn't want to get jittery or spill coffee all over myself.

I heard the musical introduction, then the beginning of the show. I should have been focusing on what I wanted to say, but my thoughts were veering in all kinds of directions: *I should be home getting ready for work, not sitting here. But how many people really watch morning TV? Not many of our friends know about this, so maybe no one will see us.*

We sat and waited, and then the director and the cameras were pointing at us. We could hear the intro we'd taped the day before, then Meredith Vieira began to ask us questions through our earbuds. We couldn't see her; we could only look into the unblinking eye of a black camera about thirty feet away. We'd been much more relaxed when we were talking face-to-face with Amy Robach in the preinterview.

Almost without warning, we were finished. I was surprised to realize it was about the time I usually began my day at school. I felt as if we'd already put in a full day's work plus overtime.

Yet this day wasn't like any other. Paul changed his clothes and went to his job, but I stayed home. Though I was tired, I thought I could work off some nervous energy by cleaning the house. Besides, I didn't often have an opportunity to do it without the girls underfoot. After a couple of hours of peaceful quiet, the phone began to ring. I spoke to a few friends who'd been shocked to see us on TV—and realized that nearly everyone I know watches early morning TV. Eventually I stopped picking up and simply let people leave messages.

I was standing in my kitchen, drinking a cup of coffee and thinking that I needed to get some work done, when the phone rang again. This time the caller was Carolyn, who told me that the media had been contacting them all day.

"Just a minute," I told her. "Someone's knocking on my front door."

"Wait," she said, "don't answer the door."

But the warning came too late. I opened the door and saw two reporters from one of the local papers on my front step. They introduced themselves and asked if they could ask me a few questions.

Was doing the Today *show a mistake?*

"We don't have anything else to say," I told them.

"We're going to run a story whether you say anything or not," the reporter answered. "You talked with the *Today* show today."

Then she began to fire questions at me: What was the name of my fertility clinic? Could they take my photo? Could they come inside and talk?

Ellen had advised me not to go public unless I was prepared to face the media. I thought I was. I was ready to field phone calls and e-mails, but I wasn't ready to handle reporters at my front door.

Finally I said, "I'll think about this. What's your number? I'll consider speaking over the phone."

Later that afternoon I participated in a few telephone interviews. I gave the reporters only the most basic information, thinking that if I gave them the bare facts they'd be satisfied and leave us alone. I went back into the house and closed all the blinds, then remembered to lock the doors.

The following hours were some of the scariest of my life. Instead of quickly dying, the story seemed to pick up momentum and my phone kept ringing. A couple of television producers left a message and asked for interviews later in the week.

"We can't," I stated firmly. "Thank you for the invitation, but the baby is due soon."

Reporters descended on our house, lining the curb with their cars and remote broadcast vans. When I didn't answer the door, some of them went back to their vehicles, where they sat, waiting. Reporters crowded around our front step and the back door, even trying the knob. Inside the house, I stared at the jiggling doorknob and wondered what I had gotten myself into. What were these people doing? I didn't want to do any more media. I didn't want people at my house. Had I inadvertently put my kids in danger? What would I have to do to call off the media hounds?

Paul was at work while all this went on, so I remained alone, a prisoner in my own home. Because an occupied, unmarked SUV had been parked across the street from my house for two hours, I called the nonemergency number for our local police and briefly explained our situation. They came out, and I asked them if they could do something to clear away the reporters. One of the officers left his business card and told me to call whenever I felt unsafe.

All day long I answered phone calls and e-mails. I tried to be brief and accurate in my responses to questions, and I realized that in one day we had shared our lives with what felt like the entire world. Did we make the right choice? How long could we have maintained our privacy if we hadn't spoken out?

That night, both Paul and I were exhausted as we fell into bed. The strain of the interview, the stress of little sleep, and the pressure of so much media attention had left us wondering if we'd made the right decision.

∾

After the world learned of our situation, I thought I would be prepared for anything, but people could still surprise me.

I remember telling one of Ellie's doctors about our mix-up at the fertility clinic. "It looks like we're going to have another baby," I concluded.

He stared at me, his brow crinkling. "And you're going to *take* the baby from this woman?"

I couldn't believe the look on his face. "Of course, it's our baby."

The doctor shook his head. "But she's carrying the baby and bonding with the child."

"But it's our child. By mistake he was transferred into her instead of me."

He shrugged. "But at that stage, it's just a few cells."

Just *cells*? No, an embryo is far more than just a few cells. "They're my cells," I answered, "and it's my child."

On several occasions I'd talked to well-meaning but uninformed people who'd said something similarly hurtful. In those situations, I always thought of something both my grandmothers used to tell me: "If you don't know what to say, don't say anything at all." The best thing anyone could say to us in a situation like ours was: "We'll pray that everything works out okay." That's honest, helpful, and kind.

But some comments tried my patience.

"At least you didn't have morning sickness." We could open a healthy savings account if we had a dollar for every time I heard that one.

"So . . . are you going to keep the baby?" (No comment required.)

"At least you didn't have to be pregnant."

Dozens of people summed up our predicament by saying, "Wow, what an easy way to have a baby!"

Our situation is anything but easy, I told myself. *And pregnancies are tough, but they're wonderful too.* But I kept those thoughts to myself. Most people didn't realize the extent of our emotional turmoil. They didn't know that for months, all we could think or dream about was our secret baby.

After the Savages' appearance on the *Today* show, a few friends sent me links to blogs that talked about us, so I read the ensuing comments. Several bloggers suggested that I act as a gestational carrier for Carolyn, because "that would only be fair," but those people had no idea how complicated these situations can be.

The week of the baby's birth, I asked Carolyn if she ever considered asking me to be a surrogate.

She quickly assured me that she'd never ask that of me. First, it would be just "too freaky," and second, I didn't meet the criteria on their list.

I blinked in surprise. "Why not?" After all, I didn't have many pregnancy complications with my girls.

She replied that they were looking for a woman who had been a gestational carrier before.

Without any further explanation, I knew why prior experience was important to Carolyn and Sean. A surrogate who has already served as a gestational carrier knows about the strong emotions that can develop during pregnancy, and she knows how to say good-bye. She wouldn't be likely to form such a strong emotional attachment to the baby that she'd have problems parting with the child after the delivery.

Plus, I couldn't be a surrogate for Carolyn any time soon because

I'd be caring for three children under three years old. Though people often suggested that idea as a solution to our quandary, it would not undo the fertility clinic's mistake.

Surrogacy, in fact, is more like a business relationship between employer and employee than a benefit of friendship. You want to engage a woman who's young, strong, and committed to the idea of providing a service, not being a mother.

Newsweek magazine reports that surrogacy was regulated in the Code of Hammurabi, dating from 1800 B.C. I found it interesting to realize that even the Old Testament records two incidents of surrogacy: when Sarai, Abram's wife, could not bear children, she enlisted Hagar for the task (see Genesis 16:1–6); and Leah and Rachel brought their handmaids to Jacob so the maids could bear children for them (see Genesis 30:1–13).[1] They may not have had pipettes and petri dishes in 1800 B.C., but apparently the practice of using a surrogate was not uncommon.[2]

Over the next few days, I read comments of all sorts on blogs: I saw evidence of compassion, disbelief, condemnation, and curiosity. Fortunately, I had braced myself for all those reactions.

But that doesn't mean the cruel and thoughtless words didn't hurt.

Chapter Seventeen

It's Time

On September 24, at eleven thirty in the morning, Carolyn called. She was on her way to the hospital, and this time they were going to deliver.

I didn't need to ask why they had decided it was time for the baby's delivery. I knew they were closely monitoring her, so if they'd decided to deliver, it meant the strain of the pregnancy was beginning to affect Carolyn's health.

This time I didn't panic. Instead relief and excitement bubbled over in my voice—I was so relieved our ordeal was finally coming to a close. "We'll be there as soon as we can," I assured her. "I have to call Paul and we have to drive down, but don't wait for us. If they need to take you into surgery early, don't feel that you have to wait until we get to the hospital."

As I hung up, I realized that this conversation was a lot calmer than the one we'd had with the false alarm on Monday night. I called Paul and told him to come home, but he said it'd take him at least half an hour to arrive.

No one but our immediate family members knew anything about the impending birth. Most people thought the baby was going to be born close to his due date, in early October. Only Paul and I knew our son would be born within hours.

Exhilarated by the thought of the baby's impending birth, I picked up the suitcase we'd packed on the night of the false alarm and put it in the van, then carried out cameras, the laptop, and extra water. Where *was* Paul?

Finally Paul arrived and put his bag in the car, then we set out for Ohio. The trip would take us an hour and a half, and I had a feeling those were going to be the longest ninety minutes of my life. Once we were under way, I called my parents. "Guess what? Today's the day."

Naturally excited, they asked us to call the minute their grandson was born.

We drove south with a sense of rising excitement and anticipation. On the way out of town, I grabbed our paper from the doorstep and was shocked to find a picture of myself above the fold, a screen shot taken from the *Today* show broadcast. The image was so blurry and indistinct I could hardly recognize myself, but maybe that would prove to be a good thing.

I read the front-page article as we drove. It felt weird to read about us in the press, but our situation was big news for our local paper. I might have worried about even more media attention, but our focus shifted to the baby. Paul and I wanted to concentrate on our son and not worry about anything else.

Carolyn had organized everything and walked us through how things would work once we arrived at the hospital. A small team would be waiting for us, and if we didn't see Sean right away we were supposed to ask for a certain individual. Only a few people knew we'd be coming, and they had set aside a private room where we could sit and wait.

When we arrived, we found the neonatal floor where our room was located. A huge nurses' station occupied the center of the space. Paul and I were trying to be discreet, so I wasn't sure whom we should talk to. A woman came over and said, "Can I help you?"

I mentioned the woman Carolyn had told us to ask for. The woman nodded. "I'm part of the team and aware of the situation," she said. "We have someone to meet with you, and they'll take you to the room."

The hospital workers were as good as their word. A woman escorted us to a small waiting area with chairs, tables, a sofa, a baby bed, and, surprisingly, a security guard outside the door. Paul sank into a chair and dozed off almost immediately, but by this time I was drowning in a tide of emotion. I tried to call Sean's cell phone, but when he didn't answer I knew he and Carolyn must be in the delivery room.

I prayed that Carolyn would have a smooth delivery without complications. I prayed that our son would be healthy. I tried walking around the room to work off some nervous energy. I paced, I looked out the window, I watched the clock. Finally I sat down, tapping my foot against the floor in a quick rhythm. I kept glancing at Paul and wondering how he could sleep at a time like this.

I leaned back in the chair, overcome by emotions I didn't expect to feel. We'd been through so much in the past few months—such highs and lows, such worries and doubts. Now that we had nearly reached the end of this road, I thought I'd be more collected and together. Carolyn was having our baby, she and Sean would have a few moments for a private hello and good-bye, and then they would bring our baby to us. They were not contesting our parental rights. We were eager to welcome our son. I knew exactly what was supposed to happen, and I thought everything would go smoothly during the operation.

Why, then, was I an emotional mess? This was something I'd never experienced before, not even with the birth of our girls. We had been excited and joyful when the girls were born, of course, but I'd been so sapped by the surgery that exhaustion and painkillers muted my emotions.

Sitting in that room with nothing to do but stare at the clock, I felt as powerless as I had on the day I learned that another woman was pregnant with our child. All of a sudden I found myself caught up in a surge of emotion. Tears began to roll down my face— I wasn't actually crying, but all the emotions I'd been experiencing began to spill over. Relief, excitement, regret, pain, and even a touch of jealousy mingled together as I contemplated the birth of my son.

I was still feeling hopeful and joyful. I tried to remain cool, calm, and collected, but in those minutes of waiting everything came rushing out.

I closed my eyes and visualized everything that had to be taking place in the operating room: Carolyn would be feeling the pressure of the surgeon's hand on her abdomen, the lifting away as they took the baby from her womb. I remembered when they lifted Ellie above the drape and let me see her for the first time and how she cried out—

That's when it really hit me: *I'm not there.* I will never hear Logan's first cries, I will never be the first one to see him, I will never behold him all goopy from birth or see him open his eyes for the first time.

My eyes welled with hurt, and fat, sloppy tears ran down my cheeks. All the emotions I'd been feeling for the past eight and a half months came pouring out. Yes, I was grateful for Carolyn's sacrifice, and I had thanked God every day for protecting our child. But I was missing out on his birth, and I'd never be able to tell him what I was thinking when he slid into the world or how his father reacted in that instant.

How easy it is to slip into self-pity. Maybe I should stop feeling sorry for myself and focus on what I was being given—a son.

I'd tell him how thrilled I was when I first laid eyes on him, how he felt when I finally wrapped him in my arms. I would tell him how I'd prayed for him, how much we had loved him and looked forward to the day when we could welcome him into our home.

Paul opened his eyes and looked at me, all red-eyed and drippy. "Why are you crying?"

I blew my nose. "It's nothing."

Paul waited a moment, and then he shook his head. Maybe he understood what I was going through better than I did, because he gave me a sympathetic smile and said, "Honey, welcome to the world of dads. This is what dads do. You are one of the few women in the world who have gone through what we go through with practically every kid. We're in the dark most of the time. We sit, and smile, and wait. So you're a dad; congratulations."

I swallowed hard and realized it was almost over. Finally.

"Okay." I wiped my cheeks and straightened my spine. "Okay, we're going to have a baby."

Paul gave me a hug. I watched the clock, concerned that the delivery seemed to be taking forever.

Then the door opened and a man in scrubs stepped through the doorway. Sean! He entered with several nurses. I have no idea how many there were or what they looked like, but in an instant I saw that they were pushing an incubator. I gasped as my heart skipped a beat, and at the sound of my gasp they stopped in midstride.

"Come on," I said, standing. "Oh my goodness, come on in!"

The next few moments are nothing but a blur in my memory. I remember gasping, and Paul says I was hysterical. Maybe I was, but more pent-up emotions came pouring out and I didn't care who saw what a mess I was. I resisted a sudden urge to jump up and down. I cried, Sean cried, and Paul beamed at the swaddled infant in the incubator. Our son wasn't hooked up to any wires or breathing tubes, so he was breathing on his own. His color was good; his skin a rosy pink; and a fringe of dark hair edged the cap on his head. Our son—our beautiful, perfectly healthy baby boy—was finally with us.

The repressed emotions of an entire pregnancy exploded in the first few moments of meeting my son.

I'm not a huggy person, but I threw my arms around Sean and thanked him. Then a nurse lifted the baby up and handed him to me. I held Logan in my arms and struggled through tears to ask about Carolyn.

"She's doing okay," Sean said.

"Thank you, thank you." Both Paul and I kept repeating the phrase.

"Five pounds, three ounces," a nurse said, smiling. "His Apgar score was a nine/nine."

Amazing! A strong, healthy baby at thirty-six weeks.

We got to hold him right away and help give him his first bath. The nurses measured the baby (18.25 inches), and we spent a lot of time taking pictures.

Sean and Carolyn had thought of everything. A friend of theirs had recorded Logan's first few minutes in the delivery room and was now taking pictures.

We thanked Sean again, then Paul and I cuddled our new son, overcome with a mixture of joy and gratitude. We called my parents, who were home with the girls. We told them the baby had arrived, but asked them not to call anyone yet. We'd let them know tomorrow when the court order would give us the authority to fill out his birth certificate and he would be legally ours. Paul called his mother; I called my sister. The family celebration had begun.

Then Sean and the nurses left us alone with Logan and gave me a bottle filled with formula. I took the bottle and frowned—for an instant, I forgot how to feed a baby. My mind was so overwhelmed with thoughts and feelings and the sheer power of the experience.

The previous eight months had been incredibly stressful, but Logan had arrived safely so our ordeal would soon be drawing to a close. We thanked God that the baby was healthy and Carolyn had come through the surgery well.

And as I held our baby and gave him his bottle, I realized that I would have to build memories from this moment on.

We were looking forward to a normal life with our daughters and new baby boy.

∼

At about seven o'clock that night, Sean and Carolyn came to see us. They brought Carolyn in her bed because she was still heavily medicated, but she was able to talk to us (though later she wouldn't remember the meeting). Ever the charming hostess, she kept asking if our room was all right, if we were comfortable, if we needed anything. She had arranged everything for us, so we kept expressing our gratitude and assuring her that everything was fine.

Because she hadn't been able to see much of the baby after delivery, we put him in her arms while Sean videotaped their first face-to-face meeting. She held Logan and talked to him; she studied his nose and hair and fingers and toes. I knew she had to be reliving all those months of caring for him in the way only an expectant mother can. This was the first time she'd had a chance to get a good look at the baby that had been only a grainy black and white image on an ultrasound.

Carolyn was thrilled that even though he was a preemie, Logan didn't have to go to the neonatal intensive care unit. I could tell she felt a huge sense of relief and accomplishment that she had done the best job she could possibly do. She had delivered to us a perfect, beautiful, healthy baby boy. We were all relieved, and Paul and I were so thankful. We felt blessed that everything had worked out so well.

Though we still didn't understand why God could possibly have arranged our son's birth this way, we were also thankful to him for taking what could have been a tragic situation and bringing good out of it.

∽

Paul, Logan, and I spent the night in our makeshift waiting room. We phoned a few family members and learned that the media had been calling them to find out details about the baby. We cautioned them to keep quiet because we didn't want his birth to be public information. For the first time since his thawing and transfer, we felt as though we controlled our son's fate. We were now responsible for him, and more than anything, we wanted to protect him.

At the hospital that night, Paul and I relaxed for the first time in a week. Our little room didn't have a bed, but it had everything we needed to communicate. We had lugged our phones and cameras from the car, so we were able to stay in touch and record our first few moments with our son. With my camera and laptop, I was able to send baby pictures to our family members.

Anytime we left our little room, a hospital security guard went with us. I didn't leave much, preferring to stay put. Paul went out a couple of times in search of something to eat, and encountered no problems with reporters.

Once, in the elevator, Paul felt a tap on his shoulder. He turned and saw an older woman who placed her finger across her lips and said, "Shh. We'll talk when we get off the elevator."

Paul felt like he was on an undercover operation making contact with an unknown operative. Then he stepped off the elevator and the woman introduced herself as Carolyn's mother.

Early the next morning, just before sunrise, a nurse stopped in to see us and said we needed to take Logan to the nursery for a well-baby checkup. With our security guard in tow, we walked down the long hallway and stopped into a little room for a quick exam. After the doctor examined the baby, the nurse mentioned that Carolyn wanted us to come by her room.

We were happy to go see her, and she looked better than she had the night before, when the pain medications had left her groggy. She held the baby, and while she smiled and cooed at Logan, we talked about how smoothly everything had gone. Our secret was still intact, and no reporters were in sight.

But while we were talking, her phone rang. Smiling, Carolyn picked up the phone and murmured hello, then I heard her gasp. "Are you sure, Mom? That can't be." The caller was Carolyn's mother, who told her that the *Today* show had announced the baby's birth.

We were all stunned. The four of us had told only a handful of people about Logan's birth, and they had all been sworn to secrecy. We couldn't believe the hospital staff had leaked it. Furthermore, we were all registered under false names: Carolyn and I were "Diane Strick" and Logan's wristband said, "Baby of Diane Strick." Only a handful of people were taking care of Carolyn and Logan, and they all knew to keep quiet. Carolyn said no one in their family would tell the press, and they hadn't yet shared the news with everyone in their extended family.

Sean narrowed his eyes thoughtfully and wondered aloud if the news might have come from the public relations firm they'd hired. He pulled out his cell phone and made a couple of calls, then hung up and gave us an abashed look.

He apologized, explaining that he and Carolyn had planned to release a statement after we left the hospital, but it had been sent out too soon. Paul and I accepted his apology, and at first we didn't think it was a big deal. But later I had to explain to friends and family that I had no idea there'd be a press release, so I had no idea a broadcaster would announce Logan's birth before we had a chance to call.

One of my girlfriends left a message on my phone: "Congratulations on the baby . . . though it was strange to find out about it on the *Today* show."

Paul's sister received a call from her fiancé: "Wendy, they just announced the baby was born."

Many of our friends and family heard the report on the morning news . . . and we wish they'd heard it from us. My cousins, aunt, and uncle heard the television announcement, and they weren't too thrilled about learning the news from a broadcaster. We wanted to call everyone personally, but the national media beat us to the punch.

We were surprised to learn that Carolyn and Sean wanted to issue a statement—we'd planned on sending out birth announcements, but nothing more than that. When we heard the Savages' plans, however, we told them we wanted to be well away from the area before the media descended. We still needed a court order officially declaring that Paul and I were the baby's legal parents, so once that was settled, perhaps we could come up with some kind of statement. But we wanted to wait before saying anything to the media.

After our visit with Sean and Carolyn, Paul and I took Logan back to the room set aside for us. Around noon, our son had his infant hearing test. We were anxious to receive the results, but Logan passed the test with no problem. The news relieved and delighted us.

We had told Sean and Carolyn that if their family and friends wanted to see the baby, they would have unlimited access. They called and told us their kids were coming to the hospital around twelve thirty, so could we bring the baby to Carolyn's room? After some consideration, I thought it best that a nurse take Logan up to see them. After all, Carolyn and Sean never really had a private time to say hello and good-bye to the baby they'd sheltered so many months. Their entire family had been affected by this pregnancy, and I didn't want to intrude on a private moment.

So we asked the nurse to tell Sean to give us a call when they were ready. The Savage family ended up spending about an hour and a half with Logan, saying hello and good-bye in one sweet session. Then we joined them in Carolyn's room, where we spent half an hour reminiscing and taking more photos.

Paul and I had been waiting on the Savages' lawyer, and she arrived a little later than we expected. We signed some paperwork Ellen had prepared and she took it to court, then returned at four with the court order. We would now be allowed to exercise our parental rights in preparing the birth certificate. Not until that hour on the second day did we have the legal right to make choices about Logan's care.

What a relief to know he was legally, officially, and finally ours. Now we could take our son home. But before we could leave the hospital, the baby had to be circumcised, pass the car seat test, complete the PKU test, and be released by the doctor.

While we waited, media requests continued to come in through telephone and e-mail, but all we wanted was to spend time with our son away from the cameras. We had yet to decide if we wanted to share him with the world.

At six o'clock we were still waiting for Logan's official release when Sean and Carolyn came to our room. Sean brought Carolyn down in a wheelchair, and on her lap she carried a lovely treasure chest. She offered Paul the wooden box and said it was a gift filled with a few things they wanted to share with the baby.

Paul was going to open it right then, but I knew I'd get emotional if I started to go through those precious gifts. I asked Carolyn if she minded if we opened it later, and she was fine with that. I'm sure she understood.

Once more we thanked Sean and Carolyn for all they had done for us and finally left the hospital at about seven. Our security guard escorted us through a side exit, and a car led us to the expressway. We had been dreading a confrontation with reporters, but we left without any media attention whatsoever. After a three-hour drive, we would be at my parents' house.

After leaving the hospital, we issued the following statement to the press:

> Paul and Shannon Morell are pleased to announce the birth of their baby boy. He was five pounds, three ounces, and eighteen inches long. We're looking forward to introducing him to his older sisters and family. It's been a long, difficult journey, and we're thrilled that our family is now complete. We will be eternally grateful for his guardian angel, Carolyn Savage, and the support of the entire Savage fam-

ily. We appreciate all the prayers and support. We're looking forward to spending the next few weeks getting to know our new baby. We ask that the media respect our privacy as we move forward.

As I peered at our sleeping baby in his car seat, I couldn't help wondering: What would be the quickest route back to normalcy?

∾

We were anxious to introduce Logan to our family and let our girls meet their baby brother for the first time. When we walked up to the front door, my mother looked out and said, "He's really yours?"

"He is," Paul answered. "And we have the paperwork to prove it."

Megan was excited and wanted to hold him. Usually we have a hard time getting her to sit still and smile, but she was happy to sit still if it meant she could hold Logan. Ellie seemed to think he was a little doll and was amazed when he opened his eyes.

A sense of quiet and peace reigned over my parents' house that first night, despite the occasional wails of a newborn baby. I showed my parents the court order and told them about the encounter I had when I went to complete the birth certificate at the hospital. The woman who handles those matters made a quip: "Must be nice just to come to the hospital and pick up your baby."

I know she probably didn't mean to be insensitive, but the remark stung nonetheless. I looked at her and said, "Trust me, it wasn't all that easy."

Now that we had our baby, I was ready to accept our friends' congratulations. Away from the hospital, far from the reporters and cameras, things finally began to feel right. At long last, we could enjoy normal interactions with our children. We could rest in the knowledge that this child was physically and legally our responsibility to care for and love.

Paul's mom came up the next day and spent time with Logan. Life slowly shifted back to normal, but several times I had to explain to friends and relatives why some of them learned about Logan on a morning news program.

The next week, after Paul and I had gone home, my mother drove down and brought me flowers. I held the bouquet of delphinium and other spring blossoms in my arms and breathed deeply of their sweet scent. Carolyn deserved the flowers, not me. She did all the hard work.

But the beautiful arrangement warmed my heart.

With a new baby in the house, I was tired and sleep-deprived. All I wanted was for my life to return to an even keel. A child is tiny for only so long, then those days are gone and we can never get them back.

Chapter Eighteen

Hello and Good-bye

Two days after Logan's birth, when I was home and all three children were resting quietly, I opened the treasure chest the Savages had given us as we prepared to leave the hospital. I had suspected this box would provoke tears, and it did.

Inside, Carolyn and Sean had placed a new pair of baby Nikes, a tiny preemie outfit, and a couple of baby hats. I lifted out a small basketball and copies of *Goodnight Moon, Brown Bear, On the Night You Were Born,* and *Baby Giggles.* They had thoughtfully included a framed picture of Logan's first moment outside the womb, with Sean holding him and Carolyn looking on. They had ordered a beautiful blanket with a heartfelt message embroidered on the edge, and every time I read it, I would thank God for their kindness.

I wiped tears from my eyes, folded the blanket neatly, and added Logan's hospital bracelet to the special treasures in the chest. I would value this gift always, for my son's sake.

&

Now that our son is safe and at home, our family is complete. We love Logan to death, and Paul calls him his "little buddy." His mannerisms and facial expressions frequently remind us of different family members.

After the birth, Carolyn told me that people sometimes asked her, "What if you'd never heard about the mistake and you had kept this child? Would you know he's not genetically yours?"

She replied that she didn't know. Sean came from a large family, so she couldn't say whether she'd have realized there'd been a mistake.

Each child is different, of course, but Logan definitely looks like Ellie—in fact, she'll point to her own baby pictures and say, "Logan." Even if we hadn't done DNA tests, we would know he belongs to our family.

At the time of this writing, the last nine months have been the most difficult months of my life. I've been on a wild roller coaster, and at some point Paul and I have felt every possible emotion. I desperately wanted to keep our situation private, but at the same time, I wanted to share the amazing and happy news that we were expecting a son. I wanted to be happy that the Savages agreed early on to give our child to us, but I was torn apart by worry about the baby's and Carolyn's health. A host of conflicting desires constantly pushed and pulled at me.

I've felt guilty that I wasn't able to love and talk to my son in utero, as I had with my girls. I've felt guilty because Carolyn had to carry my baby. I've felt robbed because I didn't have one last opportunity to feel a baby move or respond to the sound of my voice.

Before this situation, I never realized how much joy I got out of sharing my pregnancy with friends and family. Before the birth, this pregnancy was anything but joyful. Even though we were cautiously optimistic, we never knew the joy we'd experienced with our girls.

But we prayed and cheered for our little baby every week. Adoptive parents certainly go through a situation similar to ours, but they sign on for that experience and know what to expect. Our dilemma was forced upon us; we had no choice in the matter.

Because I couldn't feel free to talk about the situation uppermost in my mind and heart, I cut myself off from friends in whom I usually confide. For weeks I even isolated myself from family members.

Nothing could prepare me for the empty feeling I experienced. Worst of all, I could find no books to read for comfort, no similar stories to read for advice and practical tips. Our situation was unique; we were reluctant pioneers in the field of embryonic mishaps.

Despite all those confused and troubling feelings, Paul and I have made peace with what happened. We believe that everything happens for a reason, and for some reason God wanted another woman to carry our child. Why? I can't say for certain, but one day I trust we will completely understand.

And how will we tell Logan about his unusual arrival? We've decided that the only way to prevent him from being shocked by the story is to do what many adoptive couples do—we will make the story of his miraculous homecoming a regular bedtime story, so he and his sisters will grow up hearing his birth story along with theirs. Early on, all our children will learn that God works in amazing ways to bring families together.

I know we become stronger when we deal with difficult situations, and I know this experience has taught me to develop a thicker skin and a stronger faith. And who can forget the greatest blessing? Out of this trial came a beautiful baby boy who looks a lot like his grandpa Savage.

When reflecting on our experience, Paul says it is odd to think of Logan as frozen in time, but that's exactly what he was. "I've always felt he was trying hard to get to us, to make this journey. You could almost feel the will of this plucky little embryo. He survived the freeze and the thaw, and he came from the same batch of eggs and sperm that originated Ellie and Megan. In a sense, they're the same age, but Logan was born almost three years after they were.

"Sometimes it disturbs me when doctors don't think of embryos as anything more than clusters of cells. They're so clinical; sometimes they can seem heartless. You have to realize what we did—those embryos are little people, they contain a complete genetic code, and they're human. Logan stayed put and came back to us after all that time—through a miracle, he found a way to get into his daddy's arms. He's a persistent little guy . . . I think he must get that trait from his mama."

Paul says he will always be thankful to Sean and Carolyn for the gift they gave us. "I heard," he says, "that some people urged Carolyn to 'undo' the mistake by aborting the pregnancy. But if someone had handed her the wrong baby in the nursery, would she have 'undone' the mistake by tossing the baby in the trash? No . . . and Logan was no less human, no less a life worthy of protection. Carolyn and Sean were our only line of defense for our baby, so that makes them heaven-sent defenders. Or loving life givers. But whatever you call them, we'll always be indebted to them for protecting Logan's life."

Acknowledgments

We'd like to thank our team: Mary Martin, Angela Hunt, and Cindy Lambert. This book was truly a collaborative effort. We appreciate all your insight, input, and friendship along the way.

Last fall, we received a call from producer Mary Martin, of Blackbird Fly Entertainment. Our story had intrigued her, and she thought others would benefit from us sharing our experience. Though we hadn't considered writing a book, she convinced us we should. From beginning to end, Mary, as our book consultant, devoted hours upon hours of her time and energy to the project. Not a day went by that we didn't exchange a phone call or e-mail. She worked on this book as if it was her own, and for that, we thank her. At our house, she'll always be "Auntie M."

Thank you, Angie Hunt! I'm so glad you agreed to collaborate with us on this book. We're truly grateful for your interest in reproductive technology and protecting the life of the unborn. I sincerely hope our effort to reveal the misconceptions of in vitro will begin a dialogue throughout the world. Thanks for your patience and, most of all, for your dedication to this project.

To Cindy Lambert, our editor, you were great to work with. We could always expect a calm voice on the other end of the phone, and your words were always encouraging. We appreciate your sharp editing and vision for this book. Thank you for your tireless work.

Many thanks go to Jonathan Merkh, vice president and publisher of Howard Books, not only for championing our story but for seeing it with such clarity from day one.

To Becky Nesbitt, Jessica Wong, and Jennifer Willingham: thank you for your support.

Thank you to our manager, Alan Gasmer, of Alan Gasmer and Friends, for making our little family feel so very protected. You have had our backs every inch of the way. We are so very blessed to have you in our lives.

To Ellen Essig, our attorney, who provided invaluable legal counsel. She always promptly returned phone calls and assured me from day one that we'd be able to secure our parental rights. We're so thankful!

To our parents, thank you for letting the girls spend many weekends with you. I don't know who had more fun, them or you! You've always been supportive of anything we've undertaken, but we would never have been able to complete this book without your love and support.

To our friends and family, thank you for your kindness and

prayers. Many of you wondered why we didn't share the news sooner, and we thank you for your understanding.

In the end, this book could never have been written if it weren't for Sean and Carolyn Savage. Though it's hard to know what the future holds for all of us, our hope is that Logan will always know who you are, and when the time's right, we'll tell him about 2009 and that his birth was a blessing. Though 2009 was a difficult year for all of us, we all tried to give him the best start at life that we could. Now it's his turn to go out into this world and become a man who lives a purposeful life, thanks God daily for his blessings, and makes us all proud. Thank you for nurturing our son, protecting him, and most of all, loving him enough to let him go.

References and Resources

Resolve provides information to families who are struggling with infertility as well as workshops on the legal, medical, and mental health aspects of reproductive technologies. http://www.resolve.org.

The website http://www.creatingafamily.org offers information on infertility and adoption, including international adoption. The site also features several topical radio programs you can listen to online.

For Christian couples interested in donating or adopting embryos, you can find information at http://www.nightlight.org. You can find additional information at http://www.embryoadoption.org.

Those who are interested in donating embryos to science for stem-cell research should read the article at this site: http://www.cbhd.org/stem-cell-research/overview.

Stephanie TeSlaa of Miracles Photography: www.miraclesphotography.com.

Attorney Ellen Essig's Web site can be found at http://www .surrogatesearch.com.

Parents who have lost a little one either during pregnancy or shortly after birth may be interested in the services offered by http://www.nowIlaymedowntosleep.org. This group of professional photographers will do their best to create a lovely, lasting memory of your precious baby.

Appendix A: The Pros and Cons of IVF

Since we have gone public with our story, we have a greater awareness of why people are opposed to in vitro fertilization. Though
Paul and I are still strong advocates of in vitro, we do question the
methods clinics use to grade embryos. When you are caught up in a
desire to have children, and when your doctor assures you that any
embryos not implanted can be frozen and preserved, everything
sounds logical and sound.

Paul and I went through only one in vitro cycle. I asked many
questions; I thought I was being proactive and remaining on top of
things. I did a lot of research, and I thought we were being especially vigilant to make sure any embryos we created were not discarded.

Because the clinic I used came so highly recommended, what
I didn't do was enough research into questions regarding embryonic life. People need to ask specific questions about success statistics, but they also need to ask how doctors evaluate embryos. How

many embryos will they watch? Do they watch for two days, three, or five? What happens to embryos that are still alive but might be "substandard" or fragmented? (Fragmented embryos can result in perfectly healthy babies.)

As we waited for Logan to be born, Paul and I pondered the difficulties and the blessings of reproductive technology. Something my doctor said during that first eventful meeting in his office kept haunting me—he had told us that the three Morell embryos Carolyn's doctor transferred into her womb were "low quality," adding that if he'd been the doctor in charge, he wouldn't have recommended transferring them.

After Logan's birth, an epiphany struck me like the cut of a whip. If my doctor had been in charge, he might have discarded those "low quality" embryos, including the one that developed into our precious and perfectly healthy baby boy.

What? I had been a champion of in vitro, I had trusted my doctor, placed my faith in him, and told him of my conviction that no human lives should be wasted or destroyed in our procedures. Yet by stating that he wouldn't have recommended transferring those embryos, he was tacitly admitting that he might have denied Logan a chance to live.

By what authority can a doctor determine whether another human life has the right to exist?

If I were an in vitro patient today, my choices would depend upon the wording my doctor used with me, his patient. If he said my embryos were fragmented, I might think they were falling apart and dying. If he said they were "not doing well," I'd think they were on the verge of death.

That's why it's so important for patients to be educated. When you choose a fertility doctor, make sure he or she values life in the same way you do.

After learning to view the bigger picture, I understood at least part of what God had accomplished in this peculiar dilemma: if *my* doctor had thawed my embryos, Logan might not be with us. In that moment, I felt unspeakably *grateful* for God's unexpected plan. Overwhelmingly thankful that God's divine intervention had protected our child.

I don't know what God has in mind for Logan—maybe he's going to discover a cure for cancer, or maybe he's going to grow up and be a hard worker and a good man (the world could use a few more of those). I don't know what he'll become, but I'm hoping he'll do good, and I know his life has a purpose. God has a plan for him, for me, for all of us.

Seeing the bigger picture has helped us make sense of all our confusion.

If I were undergoing in vitro today, I wouldn't ask about the quality of my embryos. My only question would be "Are they alive?" And if the answer was yes, I'd insist that they all be transferred to the safety of my womb. Knowing what I now know about the survival rate of frozen embryos, I would ask if my eggs, not my embryos, could be frozen for future use. I would then ask that fewer eggs be fertilized in each cycle.

I know I'd be dealing with greater expense . . . but if we believe embryos are human lives (and how can anyone deny it?), how can we be responsible and do otherwise?

A woman undergoing in vitro has to rely on the expert opinion of her doctor, because few of us have the training or the time to learn everything about fertilization and reproduction and cellular biology. That's why I urge women to find a doctor who honors and respects embryos as individual lives, not merely clumps of cells. Find a doctor who will respect your pro-life position and honor your requests.

The authors of *Basic Questions on Sexuality and Reproductive Technology* believe that in vitro can fit within ethical parameters: "Each embryo *can* be reverenced and treated with dignity,"[1] they say. Moreover:

> there are some significant choices to make regarding how in vitro is done that can alter the ethical acceptability of the procedure. These decisions should be addressed with a fertility specialist who will respect and support your theological and philosophical views. Limits can and should be placed on the number of eggs fertilized, the number of embryos reimplanted [transferred], and the fate of frozen embryos (if this avenue is taken). In light of the special importance of embryonic life, you will want to avoid selective reduction after implantation, i.e., the

destruction of extra embryos to enhance the survivability of the remaining embryos. It is similarly unacceptable to transfer so many embryos into the uterus that the likelihood of all the embryos implanting is significantly diminished. One good approach is to transfer two or three. Whether or not some of the embryos produced are to be frozen, the total number of eggs fertilized should *not* be higher than the number of children you are willing to have.[2]

I don't regret undergoing in vitro, nor do I condemn the technology. My children are proof that it can work, but my unborn children—the embryos that died or were discarded—are proof that better guidelines need to be in place. In vitro fertilization can be carried out in a safe, effective way, but patients must be educated and know how to ask the right questions.

If you are considering any type of assisted reproductive technology, I hope you will ask several pointed questions when you are ready to select a clinic and lab. The issues are crucial because they are matters of life and death.

If you will be creating embryos, be sure the clinic will allow you options if you have embryos left over. Ask them to define which options they allow, and if you will be allowed to quickly freeze any embryos that are not immediately transferred. (The faster embryos are frozen, the higher their survival rate.) Better yet, ask if they are willing to fertilize only two or three *eggs,* so that fewer embryos are risked in the process.

If a doctor is evaluating your embryos after a few days of growth, don't allow yourself to be confused by talk of "quality" or "fragmentation." Ask if the embryos are *alive.*

More stringent guidelines for in vitro clinics loom on the horizon, and some clinics have come up with programs to encourage the creation of fewer embryos during a cycle. For instance, couples considering in vitro should be aware of a new procedure known as eSET: elective single-embryo transfer.

Robert Stillman, medical director of the Shady Grove Fertility Center, wrote in the *Fertility and Sterility* journal that finances have a lot to do with the occurrence of multiples through in vitro. Because in vitro is expensive, people tend to transfer more embryos, a situation that results either in multiples or in the loss of many embryonic lives. His clinic has instituted a "shared risk" program in which couples pay a flat fee (approximately twenty thousand dollars at the time of this writing) for up to six in vitro cycles. If they don't end up with a baby, they get their money back. This sort of program, while initially expensive, relieves some of the pressure for couples to try to get the most "bang for their buck," and results in fewer multiples. Stillman reports that patients with insurance coverage or those in the "shared risk" program are more likely to opt for eSET.[3]

The high cost of caring for preemies and high-risk pregnant patients has forced insurance companies that cover in vitro to put limits on their coverage. And in the Netherlands, while the number of transferred embryos is not restricted, the national health care insurance will not reimburse expenses if more than two embryos are transferred.[4]

Many countries and several American states have begun to limit the number of embryos that can be transferred at any one time. Legislators in Missouri and Georgia have introduced bills requiring doctors to follow the American Society for Reproductive Medicine's guidelines regarding embryo transfers.[5]

The ASRM's guidelines are based on patient age because the quality of a woman's eggs decreases as she ages. So the older a woman is, the more embryos are allowed to be transferred—for instance, patients under thirty-five are allowed to transfer one or two embryos, but women forty or over are allowed to transfer up to five.[6]

Dr. Michael J. Tucker, of Georgia Reproductive Specialists, writes: "The need to reduce embryo production initially may prompt the limited insemination of fresh oocytes [eggs], with the surplus being stored frozen as eggs for future use, rather than freezing surplus embryos after fertilization. This is already being undertaken by some couples who have ethical and moral objections to embryo freezing."[7]

Because the process of freezing is dangerous for embryos, it's not uncommon for only half of them to survive the thaw. Freezing eggs, therefore, is a more ethical option than freezing embryos. If a couple has two or three children and decides they don't want more, discarding eggs is not at all like discarding a human embryo. (Unfortunately, the freezing of eggs is more complicated than that of freezing sperm and embryos, and technology is still in development.[8])

I later learned that embryos are frozen in "straws," three to a straw. Since that's true, why did they thaw all six of my embryos at once? Why didn't they thaw three and leave the other three frozen? If they had, if they had offered the *choice*, I might have embryos remaining today.

It's important for couples investigating IVF to inquire about security protocols that are supposed to prevent mix-ups like ours. One clinic I read about online has impressive security: all patients have designated storage spaces within a tank, and the straws that hold their embryos are color-coded and labeled with unique identifying information: the patients' full names, date of birth, Social Security numbers, and the number of embryos in each straw. Furthermore, before a straw can be removed, two embryologists must examine the straw, compare it with a patient chart, and sign off on the removal.[9]

I don't understand everything about reproductive technologies, and I don't claim to be an expert on bioethics or medical science. But sometimes I find myself thinking about our embryos that failed to thrive. Would they have developed better if they had been allowed to grow in my uterus? Would we have been better off—not statistically, but ethically—if we had fertilized only three or four eggs and transferred them immediately?

I know these considerations can be confusing. I know that when your arms are empty and your heart is yearning for a child to love, it's easy to focus on the goal instead of the method. But if Paul and I could do things over again, we would definitely do some things differently.

We are not opposed to technology—in fact, we believe God has enabled mankind to put technology to good use. We are so thankful for the researchers who pioneered the way for cochlear implants, because Ellie wouldn't be able to hear without them. If your heart is prone to skipping beats, thank God for the pacemaker that can steady your heartbeat and prolong your life. If your eyes grow weak, be grateful for the glasses or surgically implanted lenses that can restore your sight.

Unfortunately, our society doesn't value human life—at least legally—until it is born. I can't forget that Logan had no rights and we had no rights until the moment of his birth. Carolyn had every legal right to terminate our child, and because her health was at risk, many people wouldn't have hesitated to recommend an abortion. She risked her health and her emotions, she surrendered thirty-six weeks of her life, and she left the hospital with empty arms.

We'll always think of her fondly. She performed a selfless act and gave us the ultimate gift.

Appendix B: If You Have Frozen Embryos

I can't help feeling that someone reading this book is thinking about their own cryopreserved embryos, wondering whether to save them, thaw them, or donate them to science.

If you could see how grateful we are for our children, you might think twice about throwing life away or indefinitely keeping it in storage. Ginny Scott told *Parenting* magazine that after giving birth to her children, now ages six and seven, she had one embryo remaining. After two years of wavering between options, she and her husband decided to use the embryo to try to have another baby—her now three-year-old daughter, who changed her "whole life."[1]

Recently *Parenting* magazine shared the stories of several couples who had stored frozen embryos. The author quoted a survey of fifty-eight couples conducted by researchers from the University of California in San Francisco. According to the survey, 72 percent of these couples remained undecided about the fate of their stored embryos.[2]

If a couple does not want to enlarge their family, the article offered four options for the parents of these tiny human lives: (1) offer them for scientific research, (2) allow the embryo to thaw without being used, (3) keep them in storage indefinitely, (4) transfer them into the mother at a time when she is not likely to get pregnant, or (5) donate them to an infertile couple for embryo adoption.

Paul and I could never endorse the first four options. Despite their small size, embryos are human beings, and they should not be used for experimentation. Thawing the embryos and leaving them alone brings about death through neglect. Keeping them frozen only postpones the questions parents must answer, and transferring them into the mother when she is unable to carry them only ensures their demise. Placing the embryos back in the mother at a time when they couldn't possibly survive reminds me of the ancient Egyptian practice of tossing unwanted babies into the Nile. One act is as "natural" as the other, and the end result for the child is the same.

Embryonic adoption, however, is a feasible option being explored more frequently by couples who have investigated in vitro. Recently I read the story of one woman, Doni Brinkman, who adopted an embryo and gave birth to a baby boy. If you'd like to read her story, you can find it at http://www.jimanddoni.com/Adoption/Snowflake/About/About.asp.

Appendix C:
When Does a Person Become a Person?

Our society is divided on the question of when an unborn baby is entitled to personhood and legal protection, and our laws reflect that division. In some states, a driver who hits a pregnant woman and causes her to lose her baby can be tried for manslaughter, but that same woman could walk into an abortion clinic and freely choose to have her unborn child ripped from her womb and destroyed.

Consider all the laws that protect unborn babies. South Carolina makes it a crime to "refuse or neglect to provide the proper care and attention" so that a child "is endangered or is likely to be endangered." The state's Supreme Court has ruled that a viable unborn child—one able to live outside the mother's womb—is a person under the law and has upheld the law's use in cases against pregnant women who use drugs.[1]

The South Carolina law uses viability as the point of legal protection, but the point of viability changes as technology improves. Viability is a constantly shifting point, but surely the matter of personhood does not shift. Besides, human embryos prepared for in vitro transfer are alive while in petri dishes at the lab, so why isn't that considered a point of viability? Yes, they will die if not transferred, but a six-month-old infant will die unless someone feeds and cares for it.

Some people would say that "personhood" doesn't begin until the moment a child is born, but all the evidence suggests that individual personhood begins the moment a child is conceived. Some people will object to this idea, citing the fact that many pregnancies end in miscarriage before the mother knows she is pregnant. But as John Feinberg, Paul Feinberg, and Aldous Huxley pointed out: "This objection apparently rests on two assumptions, both of which we find dubious. The first is that there can be no person where there is a large number of deaths, and the second is that 20 to 30 percent mortality is a large portion of the population. It should be remembered that throughout most of human history 70 percent of the babies born died in infancy. Should we say that they had no souls and were not persons? Beyond these considerations, we fail to see how the objection disproves the genetic concept of personhood. Even if the argument were correct, it does not prove that the babies spontaneously aborted were not persons. It only shows that those persons were not born."[2]

Since November 2008, a group called Personhood USA has been working to pass state amendments that define a fertilized egg as a person. In its inaugural year, the organization chartered groups in more than thirty states, and several are ready to introduce legislation or ballot initiatives in 2010.[3]

The rationale behind the personhood movement is simple. According to Supreme Court Justice Harry Blackmun, who wrote the *Roe v. Wade* decision, if the "suggestion of personhood is established . . . the fetus' right to life would then be guaranteed specifically by the [Fourteenth] Amendment."[4]

Why shouldn't a fertilized egg, an embryo, be considered a person? The second day after fertilization, an embryo will have two to four cells. It is absolutely human—not reptilian, not avian, nothing less than *Homo sapiens*. It is chromosomally different from the mother and father. It is a unique individual unlike any other in the world.

The baby's gender is determined at fertilization. His heart begins pumping at twenty-one days.[5] He produces brain waves at six weeks. By week seven he is developing fingers and toes and growing teeth beneath his gums. At nine weeks a baby has fingerprints on his skin, and he will try to grasp any object placed in his hand.[6]

Unborn babies are sentient. They feel, they act, and, in their own ways, they breathe.

In the traditional Christmas story, we read of Elizabeth, mother of John the Baptist, who tells a pregnant Virgin Mary, "When I heard your greeting, the baby in my womb jumped for joy."[7] By some miracle of God, that unborn baby knew that someone special had come to visit.

God called both the prophet Jeremiah and the apostle Paul before they were born.[8]

God fashions us during the months before our births. "You

made all the delicate inner parts of my body," the psalmist wrote, "and knit me together in my mother's womb."[9]

"No other passage," writes James Eckman, "deals with the question of prenatal life so powerfully and conclusively as Psalm 139. In this wonderful psalm . . . David reviews God's power in creating life, which he expresses as God weaving him in his mother's womb. God made his 'frame,' his skeleton. Then, in verse 16, he writes, 'Thine eyes have seen my unformed substance . . .' Undoubtedly, David is referring to the embryo. If correct, then the divine perspective on life is that it begins at conception. So awesome is God's omniscience and His omnipotence that He knew all about David even when he was an embryo! This is God's view of prenatal life."[10]

Notes

CHAPTER TWO

1. BabyCenter Medical Advisory Board, "Understanding Miscarriage," BabyCenter, http://www.babycenter.com/0_understanding-miscarriage_252.bc (accessed December 14, 2009).

2. "What Is Miscarriage?" Miscarriage Support Auckland Inc., http://www.miscarriagesupport.org.nz/what_mis.html (accessed February 11, 2010).

CHAPTER THREE

1. Centers for Disease Control and Prevention, "Assisted Reproductive Technology: Home," Department of Health and Human Services, http://www.cdc.gov/ART/ (accessed November 30, 2009).

2. Scott B. Rae, *Moral Choices: An Introduction to Ethics* (Grand Rapids, Mich.: Zondervan, 2000), 149.

3. Advanced Fertility Center of Chicago, "IVF Embryo Quality Issues and Day 3 Embryo Grading After In Vitro Fertilization," Advanced Fertility Center of Chicago, Gurnee & Crystal Lake, IL, http://www.advancedfertility.com/embryoquality.htm (accessed November 30, 2009).

4. Ibid.

5. Ibid.

6. Ibid.

7. Geoffrey Sher, "Embryo Grading CGH Normal Blastocysts," IVF Authority, http://www.ivfauthority.com/2009/09/embryo-grading-cgh -normal-blastocysts.html (accessed November 12, 2009).

CHAPTER FOUR

1. NIDCD Information Clearing House, "Cochlear Implants," National Institute on Deafness and Other Communication Disorders, http://www .nidcd.nih.gov/health/hearing/coch.asp (accessed November 16, 2009).

CHAPTER SEVEN

1. Andy Newman, "Visiting Rights Denied in Embryo Mix-Up Case," *New York Times*, October 27, 2000, http://www.nytimes.com/2000/10/27/ nyregion/visiting-rights-denied-in-embryo-mix-up-case.html (accessed November 17, 2009).
2. Associated Press, "Woman Awarded $1 Million in Embryo Mix-Up," MSNBC.com, August 4, 2007, http://www.msnbc.msn.com/id/5603277/ (accessed November 17, 2009).
3. Steven Morris and Haroon Siddique, "Couple in Embryo Mix-Up May Use Payout to Try for Another Child," *Guardian*, UK, June 15, 2009, http://www.guardian.co.uk/society/2009/jun/15/ivf-wales-cardiff-blunder (accessed November 17, 2009).
4. Ibid.
5. Ibid.
6. Maggie O'Farrell, "IVF Mother: 'I Love Him to Bits. But He's Probably Not Mine,'" *Guardian*, UK, October 30, 2009, http://www.guardian.co.uk/ lifeandstyle/2009/oct/30/ivf-errors-baby-mix-up (accessed November 24, 2009).
7. Ibid.
8. Associated Press, "Embryo Mix-Ups Stun Parents in La., Ohio," September 25, 2009, available at http://www.cbsnews.com/stories/2009/09/25/ national/main5340450.shtml (accessed November 17, 2009).

CHAPTER SIXTEEN

1. Lorraine Ali and Raina Kelley, "The Curious Lives of Surrogates," *Newsweek* (April 7, 2008), 47.

2. Scott B. Rae, *Moral Choices: An Introduction to Ethics* (Grand Rapids, Mich.: Zondervan, 2000), 159.

APPENDIX A

1. Gary P. Stewart, et. al, *Basic Questions on Sexuality and Reproductive Technology: When Is It Right to Intervene?* BioBasics series (Grand Rapids, Mich.: Kregel Publications, 1998), 29.

2. Ibid., 30.

3. Rita Rubin, "IVF: Newer 'eSET' procedure reduces risk of multiple births," *USA Today,* March 3, 2009, http://www.usatoday.com/news/health/2009–03–03-invitro-fertilization_N.htm (accessed December 14, 2009).

4. Ibid.

5. Ibid.

6. Ibid.

7. Michael J. Tucker, "The Freezing of Human Oocytes (Eggs)," IVF.com, http://www.ivf.com/freezing.html (accessed January 13, 2010).

8. Pacific Fertility Center, "Why PFC?" Pacific Fertility Center, http://www.pacificfertilitycenter.com/welcome/lab_freeze.php (accessed January 12, 2010).

9. Ibid.

APPENDIX B

1. Laura Bell, "What Is the Fate of Leftover Frozen Embryos?" *Parenting,* August 27, 2009, http://today.msnbc.msn.com/id/32489239 (accessed November 19, 2009).

2. Ibid.

APPENDIX C

1. Randy Alcorn, *Prolife Answers to Prochoice Arguments* (Sisters, Ore.: Multnomah, 2000), 96.

2. John S. Feinberg, Paul D. Feinberg, and Aldous Huxley, *Ethics for a Brave New World* (Wheaton, Ill.: Crossway Books, 1996, c1993), 61.

3. Adrienne S. Gaines, "Personhood Movement Gains Momentum," *Charisma* (January 2010): 16.

4. Harry Blackmun, *Roe v. Wade,* January 22, 1973, http://www.tourolaw .edu/Patch/Roe/ (accessed December 28, 2009).

5. J. M. Tanner, G. R. Taylor, and the editors of Time-Life Books, *Growth* (New York: Life Science Library, 1965).

6. Pregnancy.org, "Fetal Development Overview," Pregnancy.org, LLC, http://www.pregnancy.org/fetaldevelopment/ (accessed November 30, 2009).

7. Luke 1:44

8. Jeremiah 1:5; Galatians 1:15.

9. Psalm 139:13.

10. James P. Eckman, *Biblical Ethics: Choosing Right in a World Gone Wrong,* Biblical Essentials series (Wheaton, Ill.: Crossway Books, 2004), 29.

About the Authors

PAUL AND SHANNON MORELL

Paul and Shannon Morell have been married for eight years. Paul is an electrical engineer and small business owner. Shannon holds a master's degree in education and currently teaches eighth grade. They live in the Midwest with their preschool-age twin daughters and their new son.

ANGELA HUNT

With almost 4 million copies of her books sold worldwide, Angela Hunt is the bestselling author of *The Tale of Three Trees; Don't Bet Against Me!* with Deanna Favre; *The Note;* and *The Nativity Story.* She has written more than one hundred books in fiction and nonfiction and has won numerous awards for her work.

Angela holds a doctorate of biblical studies in theology degree and is currently working on her doctorate of theology degree. She and her husband live in Florida with mastiffs.